generation of readers'

THE
DUCHESSES

The Story of Britain's Ultimate Steam Locomotives

ANDREW RODEN

First published in Great Britain
2008 by Aurum Press Ltd
7 Greenland Street
London NW1 0ND
www.aurumpress.co.uk

This paperback edition first published in 2010 by Aurum Press.

A catalogue record for this book is available from the British Library.

ISBN 978 1 84513 599 7

1 3 5 7 9 10 8 6 4 2

2010 2012 2014 2013 2011

Typeset by SX Composing DTP, Rayleigh, Essex
Printed in the UK by CPI Bookmarque, Croydon, CR0 4TD

Contents

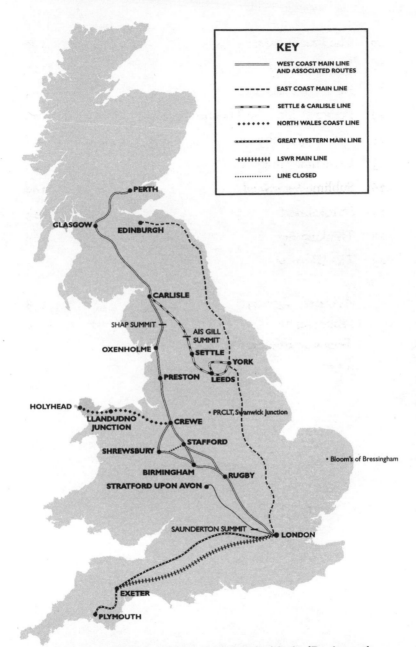

KEY

———	WEST COAST MAIN LINE AND ASSOCIATED ROUTES
– – –	EAST COAST MAIN LINE
‐·‐·‐	SETTLE & CARLISLE LINE
◆◆◆◆◆◆	NORTH WALES COAST LINE
✕✕✕✕✕✕	GREAT WESTERN MAIN LINE
++++++	LSWR MAIN LINE
··········	LINE CLOSED

PERTH

GLASGOW

EDINBURGH

CARLISLE

SHAP SUMMIT

AIS GILL SUMMIT

OXENHOLME

SETTLE

YORK

PRESTON

LEEDS

HOLYHEAD

LLANDUDNO JUNCTION

CREWE

• PRCLT, Swanwick Junction

STAFFORD

SHREWSBURY

• Bloom's of Bressingham

BIRMINGHAM

RUGBY

STRATFORD UPON AVON

SAUNDERTON SUMMIT

LONDON

EXETER

PLYMOUTH

British railways associated with the 'Duchesses'

Chapter One
Sleeping Giant

The blackout was almost complete. For the past three years, Britons had got used to the thick black curtains that prevented light from escaping through windows and alerting German pilots – but it wasn't complete everywhere. It couldn't be: some things needed light outdoors for safety, the railways chief amongst them. The signals had to be lit at night so the drivers didn't sail past a red signal, not that the light from the flickering oil lamps was particularly strong anyway. Back in 1942, Carlisle station wasn't much different from today. The roof was more complete, though vastly dirtier, there were more tracks around it, and the overhead power lines hadn't been installed – but, in essence, it was very much the same station, and it was here, on a cold spring night, that Percy Wilson, a driver at the nearby Carlisle Upperby shed, had been rostered to take over the overnight sleeper train from Perth to London. Normally, men from Crewe North shed would work out and back in a shift, but staff shortages meant that tonight it was one of Carlisle's crews instead. Sleeper carriages are heavier than normal seated coaches, but that didn't stop the railways stringing as many as possible behind the locomotive, particularly in wartime.

On the platforms, something akin to organised chaos was taking place. Porters and passengers milled about, loading the train and finding their berths. There would have been trolleys and luggage everywhere, perhaps the clang of wheeltappers, and almost certainly there would have been other trains in the busiest stations, banging and clanking as carriages were added and taken away.

Most sleeper trains ran fairly slowly in peacetime, but in wartime, the national maximum speed of 60mph, imposed to save coal and wear and tear, as well as making the most of the track capacity, meant that they were probably as fast as any others, and their morning arrival in London meant that they were often the best way for people travelling long distances to get there. They were also the heaviest passenger trains in Britain, and demanded locomotives with both power and endurance to operate for many hours without the fire clogging up with ash while still maintaining time. On the main London to Glasgow railway, the West Coast Main Line, that meant that the most powerful locomotives in the London Midland & Scottish Railway's fleet, the imposing 'Princess Coronations' – better known by many as 'Duchesses' – were the default choice. Even Wilson was surprised by the length of the train tonight, and sure enough, as he boarded the locomotive, No. 6233 *Duchess of Sutherland*, the stationmaster approached. 'This train is overloaded, driver. You've nearly 600 tons.' It looked like it would be a long night.

In 1942, the Second World War was approaching its turning point in Europe. The Americans had just entered the war, and decisive battles in North Africa and Russia would soon start to stem the tide of Nazi Germany. Britain was battered, bruised and short of essential supplies, but it was still very much in the fight.

The railway played a vital part in the war effort, running around the clock to carry passengers and goods, and though London had borne the brunt of the Luftwaffe's unwanted nocturnal attentions, the overnight sleeper trains continued to run, taking soldiers, sailors and airmen, as well as a huge number of civilians, on their way to the capital.

Getting sleep on a sleeper train can be difficult in peacetime, so it's not hard to imagine how difficult it must have been in the war. Every sleeping cabin would have been full, and the chances were that there would have been plenty of people in the train grabbing whatever sleep they could wherever they could. Given that in the 1950s these sleeper trains were full and with people standing in corridors and seated compartments, it's difficult to imagine that it would have been any different in wartime.

Those lucky passengers asleep in their beds could have no idea of the extraordinary efforts being made at the front of the train, but for the likely majority sleeping fitfully, their journey was soon to get even less conducive to good sleep.

Duchess of Sutherland had been built in July 1938 at Crewe, one of a small batch of unstreamlined 'Duchesses' that operated alongside their streamlined sisters. Another engine in this batch, No. 6234 *Duchess of Abercorn*, had set a British power record for a steam passenger locomotive of 3,300hp in 1939 that remains officially unbeaten to this day. She was painted in wartime black, a drab scheme that did little for the looks of most locomotives. Even this, however, couldn't detract from the sense of imposing power and authority she exuded. Drab or not, she was still one of the most exciting spectacles on the rails, and all her power and might was needed on this duty.

Wilson's fireman looked over at him, a hint of concern in his face. 'Do you think we can manage, Percy?' he asked.

'With this engine, certainly,' Wilson assured him.

Wilson, and most of the locomotive crews on the West Coast Main Line, were well aware of the tremendous power of the 'Duchesses', but that power came at the cost of needing top-notch crews to get the most out of them. They pushed the loading gauge to the limit, squeezing every last inch possible under bridges and tunnels in order to have as big a boiler and firebox as possible, and, to some firemen in particular, they were as daunting as they were imposing, particularly if, like Wilson's fireman, you'd never worked on one before.

Wilson was as good as his word and, after ensuring the engine was fit to continue the journey, eased open the regulator and set *Duchess of Sutherland* on her way south. The climb from Carlisle to Shap is long and steep, and with 600 tons behind her, even this giant locomotive would struggle unless driver and fireman were on top of their game.

Although Wilson's fireman had never fired a 'Duchess' before, it quickly became clear he had the measure of the locomotive, and soon the safety valves were simmering away, indicating the boiler was full and with a full head of steam. Bit by bit, Wilson opened the regulator, taking care not to give *Duchess of Sutherland* too much throttle and make her slip, and the locomotive responded to the careful driving, speed rising up the gradient, despite the heavy load.

Perhaps those soldiers, sailors or airmen in their bunks

noticed the increasing tempo of the 'clickety clack' of the rail joints. They would surely have noticed the ride of the heavy sleeping cars beginning to lurch and bounce as speed increased. Shap was crested in thirty-one minutes – an average speed of 60mph from Carlisle – and then the loco-motive got her nose down and hared down the bank.

Duchess of Sutherland's exhaust notes merged into a con-tinuous roar, sparks flying from the chimney and the fireman shovelling coal furiously to feed her voracious appetite. The wheels beat a tattoo on the rails, and the 'clickety clack' of the carriages turned into staccato bursts like machine-gun fire. Perhaps this informed the dreams of some of the military men on the train, taking them back to places and times they'd rather forget. Perhaps it acted as a reminder that though Britain was down, she was far from out if trains could run like this. We'll never know. The locomotive and train were absolutely flying, and Wilson turned to look at the speedometer, having been concentrating hard on the line ahead. When a locomotive runs as smoothly as a 'Duchess' it can be very difficult to work out how fast one is really going, particularly at night when one only sees a blur of the objects nearest the engine. As he turned his head his eyes almost popped out. With a 600-ton load, *Duchess of Sutherland* was belting down Shap at 110mph – the same speed as an electric locomotive today. Only one 'Duchess' had verifiably done this speed before, with a light test run, and with such a heavy load, he must have asked himself if the speedometer was mis-reading. It might well have been, but only by a few miles an hour. The speed could have been anywhere between 105mph and 115mph, and, in truth, it would have made little difference. The intermediate stop between Carlisle and Crewe, Wigan, was reached seven minutes early, and from there, Crewe followed in thirty-two minutes.

The performance was electrifying. Indeed, it was so good that even now, more than sixty years on, it's unlikely to have been beaten. The sheer power of *Duchess of Sutherland*, and the skill of Wilson's hand on the regulator – and of course, his fireman on the shovel – had produced an impromptu demonstration of the locomotives that many consider to be the best ever built in Britain.

It's sometimes too easy to label achievements with superlatives, but Wilson's run, uncovered by the Chief Engineer of the Princess Royal Class Locomotive Trust, Brian Radford, deserves every plaudit that can be thrown at it. Wilson has always been adamant about the locomotive's achievement, and few who know the 'Duchesses' would reject it out of hand. It was compelling proof of the design's power and speed and epitomises what these locomotives could do when they were (all too rarely) given their heads.

To many, the 'Duchesses' were and are Britain's ultimate steam locomotives, the benchmark against which all others are judged, a benchmark that has never been equalled, yet alone beaten. But it's a bold and brave assertion to make, as in most walks of life there is always the prospect of something better, and there are serious challengers for the title amongst steam locomotives. In the field of airliners, for example, you could make the case for the Boeing 747 being the ultimate airliner for a long time, but its crown seems likely to pass to the Airbus A380 'Superjumbo'. With British steam locomotives, it's a slightly more definite question to answer as British Rail dispensed with steam in 1968. So, at that point, one can make a reasoned judgement as to what really was Britain's ultimate steam locomotive.

For me it's a question of which design achieved feats that no others did or could: the design whose nearest competitors, if put on the same duty for a prolonged period, would be found wanting. On the face of it, coming to a conclusion should be a straightforward exercise. But there's a complication to this, as, thanks to dedicated preservationists, many of the contenders for the title of 'the ultimate' survived and eventually ran on the main line at the head of enthusiasts' specials. The ultimate steam locomotive, therefore, really ought to demonstrate some kind of supremacy after fleet operation of steam finished in 1968 – and, since then, we've learnt an awful lot about the rivals of the 'Duchesses' for the throne. Were they *really* as good as many believe? That's what I set out to discover.

This book isn't intended to be a technical history of the class – there are plenty of books that really drill into the detail – but to explore the story of its design, the things that the 'Duchesses' did that make them such a potent symbol of the power of steam, and, hopefully, to bring to life some of the people over the years who have played such important parts. The story proper, though, starts from a time when their railway, the London Midland & Scottish, was having real difficulty in providing powerful enough locomotives to haul its heaviest passenger trains. In many senses, it was a railway in crisis.

Chapter Two
A Railway in Crisis

In 1932, the London Midland & Scottish Railway sat on top of Britain's railway tree. It ran the main railways from London Euston and St Pancras to the north, the line across the top of North Wales, and as far north as Thurso. It also operated ships and road fleets, and had a stake in Railway Air Services too. It employed 233,000, operated around 10,000 locomotives, 19,000 coaches and 300,000 wagons, and ran over 9,620 route-miles. It was a giant – the biggest of the four railways created in 1923 by a fair margin.

But it had problems, and most of these were caused by the bitter internal rivalries created when it was formed in 1923 as part of the 'Grouping', which rationalised the dozens of railways in Britain to just four. The LMS's three biggest constituents were the London & North Western Railway, which ran from Euston, the Midland Railway, which ran from St Pancras, and the Lancashire & Yorkshire Railway, which ran a multitude of important routes around the cities of Manchester, Liverpool, Sheffield and Leeds. The difficulty was that, in the years running up to the Grouping, the Midland on the one hand and the LNWR and LYR on the other had competed ferociously. Putting them into the same company didn't stop the competition; it simply internalised it, and whenever a decision needed to be made, each faction tried to get its way. It didn't help that their *modi operandi* were so different across the spectrum of engineering, operation and customer service.

Nowhere was this more apparent than in the provision of locomotives. The Midland Railway had believed in using small locomotives to run its trains, coupling two or three together when there were heavy loads. (It was later described, with no small degree of accuracy, as 'The Society for the Prevention of Cruelty to Engines'.) When trains were light and a single engine was able to cope there was no problem, and providing one small locomotive was cheap, but when loads got heavier, and more than one engine and crew were needed, operating got more expensive than having a single more powerful engine able to do the job. The LNWR, on the other hand, believed in having more powerful locomotives and working them hard, as did the LYR. This was in line with the policy espoused by other railways, but the Midland influence – led by the accountants – dominated in the early years of the LMS, to the detriment of passengers.

The Chief Mechanical Engineers (CMEs) were all handicapped by this 'small-engine' policy, and when new locomotives were needed, the powers that be decreed that batches of Midland-designed locomotives were what was really best. Every time the Chief Mechanical Engineer, Henry Fowler, prepared designs for new locomotives, the dead hand of Midland Railway policy slapped him firmly down, led by James Anderson, the Chief Motive Power Superintendent. By 1930, the Midland Railway designs so beloved of Anderson were long past it, and locomotive crews were struggling to meet growing demands placed on them and their charges. Still, however, the short-sighted procurement policies continued.

The situation had, partially, at least, been alleviated by the arrival in 1927 of the 'Royal Scots', which were intended for the principal London–Glasgow trains. They were far more powerful than anything else in the fleet and were able performers – but there weren't nearly enough of them, and still the complaints of engine sheds from Euston to Glasgow and Perth went unheeded. As long as the Midland Railway influence held sway, little would change, and that change was urgently needed.

It started in 1927 when the distinguished economist Sir Josiah Stamp became chairman of the company. Coming from outside the railway, and with a firm belief in improving efficiency, Stamp was able to impose an impartial policy. He immediately started planning radical change, with a two-pronged attack to sort things out. Analysis was started that would eventually lead to standardised equipment; offices and jobs would be amalgamated and rationalised; and ways of financing the improvements so desperately needed were investigated. This was the beginning of a massive restructuring programme that applied rationality to a railway that hitherto had been limited by tradition and internal conflict.

Stamp took his time before he made a real impact on locomotive engineering, but when the CME, Henry Fowler, retired in 1932, and, in turn, his successor, Ernest Lemon, was promoted, it was clear that change was in the air. When it came to deciding who to appoint next, although there were extremely capable men at Crewe, Horwich and Derby, Stamp decided to appoint from outside the company – a move that would guarantee there would be no question of partiality to any of the drawing offices.

The man he chose was the number two at the Great Western Railway, William Stanier. Stanier was born in Swindon on 27 May 1876, the son of William H. Stanier, the chief clerk to CME William Dean. From an early age, Stanier Junior enjoyed making things and was bought his first set of chisels at the age of ten. Engineering was in the young man's blood, and nobody in his family was going to discourage his learning. He joined the GWR as an office boy in 1891 before becoming an apprentice at the age of sixteen: his railway career had started.

Stanier rose through the ranks of the Great Western Railway, and was appointed Assistant to the Chief Mechanical Engineer, Charles Collett, in the early 1920s. However, just a few years separated Collett from Stanier, so if Stanier was to succeed his senior, it wouldn't be for long as the Great Western, like many railways of the time, promoted strictly on the basis of seniority.

Still, Stanier was content at the Great Western, and was highly regarded for his community activities – Collett withdrew into himself following the death of his wife, leaving Stanier to fulfil the community responsibilities expected of the man in charge at Swindon. He was a founder member of Swindon Rotary Club, a governor of Swindon Secondary School, was president of the rugby and athletics clubs, was on the boards of the Swindon Gas Company and Swindon Permanent Building Society, and was elected a JP in 1931. Stanier was very much a family man, and took a keen interest in his children, nieces, and nephews in particular. Though in work he could come across as austere and formal, in private, he was a genuinely warm and likeable man. He zipped around the works at high speed, becoming known as 'the black arrow' and from pictures you'd expect him to speak in a clipped, rapid-fire, well-to-do voice. But he didn't. Stanier was a Wiltshireman with a deep, gruff voice and a definite local twang. It was rather at odds with his appearance, all things considered.

But the LMS wasn't interested in Stanier for his personal qualities, admirable as they undoubtedly were. What it, and, more particularly, Stamp, wanted was a practical, down-to-earth, reliable engineer who could impose order on chaos, and bring proven outside experience to the company. In this respect, Stanier's credentials were impeccable. He had been instrumental in the success of the 'Castle' class express locomotives, and, as Works Manager at Swindon, had proven his understanding and engineering ability. His knowledge of what made the Great Western's fleet perhaps the best of any in Britain at the time was beyond doubt – and that fleet was what the LMS hoped to emulate.

The approach was made in October 1931. Sir Harold Hartley, Vice-President and director of scientific research, was tasked with finding a replacement for the existing CME, Ernest Lemon, who was soon to be promoted. Hartley wasn't a railwayman at all, coming as he did from a position as tutor of Balliol College, Oxford – but he had noticed the quality of operation on the Great Western, and thought Stanier would be a good candidate. He asked the LMS's former CME, Sir Henry Fowler, what he thought of Stanier. Fowler's appraisal was positive, and soon Hartley talked about water softening and boiler maintenance with Stanier at the Athenaeum over lunch. Hartley was impressed, and soon invited Stanier for another lunch. This time, Stanier sought permission from Collett, as it was becoming clear that a job offer might be in the offing. Following Collett's blessing, the lunch was had, the offer was made, and after a meeting with Stamp, the deal was sealed: Stanier would be the new CME of the LMS.

He very quickly made it clear that he would follow Stamp's brief and produce new designs that would cut costly double-heading and eliminate a large number of old, inefficient designs. Previously, Anderson had specified the number and type of locomotive he wanted, and left the engineering team to it. Because, by and large, Anderson had ordered Midland designs, there was little for the designers to do. When Anderson submitted his first request to the new CME, Stanier ignored it. After a while, Anderson asked why Stanier hadn't replied to the request. 'I am trying to decide what new locomotives are needed and can only do this if you specify the numbers and duties they are to perform,' responded Stanier. The message got through loud and clear – Anderson could request locomotives for certain duties, but it was Stanier who would decide the form those locomotives would take. Finally, the LMS had a CME willing and able to grasp the nettle and assert his authority.

Chapter Three
New Broom

The arrival of William Stanier at Euston must have sent shockwaves through the drawing offices: was his appointment a slight against them? Was it an admission that LMS practice was inferior to that of the Great Western? What on earth would happen?

For his part, Stanier had the benefit of a clear brief and great experience of the free-steaming locomotives of the Great Western. It was this that Stanier wanted to bring to the LMS, as well as reliable axleboxes. The Derby influence of locomotive design had imposed the poor Midland Railway design of axleboxes, which often had too small a bearing surface, and as a result ran hot and seized with monotonous regularity.

He knew he couldn't simply waltz in and change the way things were done wholesale – to change too much at once with designers and factories unfamiliar with other methods would be to court disaster. What he wanted to do was to develop a small range of locomotives that would cover all duties and make maximum use of standard parts. He had been involved in a similar process on the Great Western at the turn of the century, and was keen that the LMS should reap the operating and economic benefits of standardisation.

At the early 1932 meeting of the LMS Locomotive Committee, Stanier made a persuasive case for a new type of express passenger locomotive to supplement the 'Royal Scots' and 'Patriots', which held the line on the most demanding duties. He wanted a locomotive that could run 400 miles or so – the distance between London and Glasgow – without needing to be changed at Carlisle as was currently the practice. It would save money, speed journeys, and also offered the chance for non-stop runs between London and Glasgow if desired.

The board gave the go-ahead for three locomotives. It wasn't a huge order, but it was enough for Stanier to make a start. Stanier had been instrumental in the design of the Great Western Railway's 'King' and 'Castle' classes, and it was the former on which he decided to base the new LMS locomotive. The 'Kings' were giants, comfortably the biggest locomotives of their configuration in Britain, but Stanier knew that they could have been better. With four wheels in a bogie to guide them, and then six huge driving wheels putting the boiler's power onto the rails (a 4-6-0 in technical parlance), they were powerful, but their axle loads were really too high, and placed huge stress on the track. Stanier resolved to ease this by adding a small pair of trailing wheels at the rear of his new design, creating the LMS's first ever 4-6-2, or 'Pacific', locomotive. The locomotive would be powerful, and with a new wider firebox should be able to generate more steam. Crucially, by not seeking to re-invent the wheel, Stanier should be able, fairly simply, to give the LMS the high-power traction it needed so urgently.

As the new locomotive took shape on the drawing board, it was clear that it was virtually an extended 'King' with some technical changes to reflect Stanier's own preferences. The locomotive was given the number 6200 and named *The Princess Royal*. She emerged from Crewe Works in July 1933 and made an immediate impression. She was big, powerful, fast and imposing. A second locomotive, No. 6201 *Princess Elizabeth*, followed in November that year. The third was to be an experimental design and didn't emerge until much later.

The pair introduced a number of new design features to the LMS – the taper boiler, which is narrower at the front than the rear, could have been designed at Swindon by the Great Western. This, more than anything else, ushered in a new look to LMS locomotives. They were quickly put to the test, on long-distance, heavy expresses from London, and, as their size suggested, proved very powerful – but they weren't quite as good as they should have been: the proportions of the boiler were wrong, and they meant that raising steam was rather like breathing through a blocked nose. There was no way the board of directors could countenance further orders.

Stanier and his design team quickly built a succession of successful mixed-traffic and freight locomotives, but the problem of the 'Princess Royals' continued to trouble them. They tried different designs of boiler and double-chimneys, but it was only when Stanier abandoned the Great Western practice of using low-temperature superheating (where the steam is taken from the boiler and passed through the fire tubes to dry it out completely) and fitted a 32-element superheater that No. 6200 was able to perform as well as she looked.

With their performance starting to improve, funds were allocated to build another ten 'Princess Royals', though the first of these, No. 6202, was fitted with steam turbines rather than cylinders and pistons, and became known as the 'Turbomotive'. The final member of the class, No. 6212 *Duchess of Kent*, emerged from Crewe Works in October 1935.

The following year, with the 'Princess Royals' now dominating the heaviest West Coast Main Line trains, a series of tests were carried out, culminating in No. 6203 *Princess Margaret Rose* hitting 102mph (or 104mph depending on which account one believes) between Willesden and Crewe. Finally, Stanier's flagship locomotives had proved they could match pretty much anything else in Britain.

They weren't perfect, though, as Geoff Hillyard, a fireman in the 1960s, and a man who we'll meet again later in the book, recalls: for the crews, preparation was a nightmare. To oil the inside motion – the rods and levers that transferred the motion of the two pistons between the main frames to the driving wheels – one of them had to go under the locomotive, and take out the corks, fill reservoirs with oil and replace them on no fewer than twenty-seven awkwardly placed lubricating points. For all their power, the 'Princess Royals' were a servicing nightmare.

Nonetheless, by 1936, with Stanier's mixed-traffic designs now flooding into service, there was still a need for more 'Princesses', and although the design had flaws, it was the only one the LMS had. Although it doesn't seem to have been in the 1937 building programme (which was agreed on 26 July 1936), soon after that date, it was confirmed that a further five 'Princesses' would be built. The Derby drawing office, however, had different ideas.

E.A. Langridge had worked in the drawing office since 1920, and, as he put it, quoted in *The LMS Duchesses* by Douglas Doherty, 'to the discriminating eye, the "Princess" design did not seem to be using material to the best advantage. There were the four valve gears, the spread-out wheelbase, and the boiler seemed to be a long drawn-out affair.

'From technical magazines, one could see what was happening elsewhere, and felt that one could do as well or better than the others.'

Langridge wasn't alone. Tom Coleman, the redoubtable and austere Chief Technical Assistant at Derby, firmly believed that the LMS was capable of designing and building a new express locomotive that would be more powerful, more reliable and easier to maintain than the 'Princesses', while keeping to the same weight limits. Coleman approached Stanier with a 'Plan B' for the new express locomotive soon after the order for the 'Princesses' was confirmed. Coleman must have been hopeful of approval, for the new design embodied everything the LMS and Stanier had learned about locomotive design over the previous four years. 'Plan B' had bigger wheels, a boiler built to the maximum permissible limits on height and width, a huge tender – and would be built with absolute reliability and ease of maintenance in mind. Stanier looked at the design carefully: he would soon be travelling with a British delegation to report on the state of India's railways, so Coleman and the design teams would be left largely to their own devices. Could this, he asked, better the 'Princesses' at little extra cost? After careful consideration, he gave

Coleman's design his blessing, and instructed that five loco-motives must be ready for the 6½ hour London–Glasgow trains, which would start in June 1937. They would be built at Crewe.

Chapter Four
Giants on Earth

The town of Crewe revolved around the railway works. Established by the Grand Junction Railway in the 1840s, and expanded by the London & North Western Railway, by 1936 it was the heart of the LMS's locomotive-building and maintenance capability. The town was built by the railway and the railway works was one of the biggest industrial operations anywhere in the world.

It had always had a reputation for building rugged machines at low cost, but under Stanier's regime, its exquisite craftsmanship, hitherto hidden under a bushel, came to the fore. It was the right place, and probably the only one of the LMS's factories that could build the giant new locomotives that Coleman had in mind.

The LMS wanted to launch the new locomotives in a blaze of glory, and in order to disguise just how much bigger and more powerful they were than the 'Princesses' it called the new design 'Princess Coronation', a clumsy term, but one that implied the new locomotives would be refined 'Princesses'. It was a grand deception.

Manufacturing on the scale of Crewe has now largely disappeared in Britain, but one man who remembers it well is Harold Fortuna, who started work there in late 1932 at the age of fourteen. He tells a story of a factory with some surprising problems, and of a meeting with the top brass after he had mistakenly ground off some decorative chromium plating from one of the LMS's most famous engines, 5552 *Silver Jubilee*.

This was my first meeting with the legendary Roland Bond, the assistant works superintendent. Now, the top brass were getting worried about the educational level of the workers: many could not even read and write. Anyway, they decided to see this boy who had ground off all their beautiful chromium, so I was summoned to the manager's office for an interview.

Bond was one of the great locomotive engineers, a tireless advocate of improving efficiency in locomotive works, and after a career break from the LMS from 1925 to 1931, had rejoined the company, first as assistant works superintendent at Horwich, and from 1933 in the same role at Crewe.

There was Mr Bond, my head foreman, the head staff clerk, and another man who I believe was Stanier himself. The first thing Bond asked me was whether I could read and write. After I had satisfied them about that, they asked about my arithmetic, and about converting fractions to their metric equivalents, which they didn't teach in my school. I did these as my Gran had taught me, and Bond looked at the others and said, 'What the hell are you doing boy, working as a labourer?'

I told him that, as my father didn't work in the Works, I couldn't be an apprentice.

Though Bond tried to promote Harold Fortuna, he eventually said he couldn't promote him as it would create a 'precedent'. It says much that Crewe was able to produce anything at all given these constraints, never mind railway locomotives – and that it was able to be so picky about its staff seems incredible today. In more modern times, Fortuna would surely have got his promotion.

Coleman and his team at Derby were able to provide good outline drawings, and detailed design was shared with Crewe. Derby would design everything below the boiler; Crewe everything above and including it. This meant that both drawing offices played to their strengths, and as the first 'Princess Coronation' took shape on the drawing board, it was clear that the result would be a giant.

It was then that the marketing department threw what some consider to be a spanner in the works. At the time, streamlining was all the rage. It was applied to cars, ships, aeroplanes, and to trains. Stanier had investigated the usefulness of streamlining with visits to the United States and Germany, but was still far from convinced that it was worth the effort. Even with the predicted power output of the new locomotives, they still wouldn't often get above 80mph, which is around the point streamlining starts to justify the added weight and cost it adds with savings in fuel. Talking to his contemporary Oliver Bulleid (the former Chief Mechanical Engineer of the Southern Railway) in the 1960s, Stanier said, 'I asked if I could have the carapace off as I didn't think it had much real value – there wasn't any material advantage except above 70mph.'

However, by this time, the London & North Eastern

Railway (LNER) was running the famous 'Silver Jubilee' service between London and Edinburgh. At the head were streamlined 'Pacific' locomotives known as 'A4s' and they were by some measure the best express passenger locomotives in Britain at the time. The first of the type, 2509 *Silver Link*, had set a world speed record for steam of 112mph in 1935, and the carriages that formed the train were specially built to be as aerodynamic as possible, and also to incorporate the very latest developments in passenger comfort. Journey times were slashed, and there was a sense of style and glamour about the 'Silver Jubilee' that was winning business. By comparison, the LMS looked old-fashioned and slow: it had to respond if it wasn't to lose business on the London-Glasgow-Edinburgh corridor to its faster East Coast rival.

The marketing department demanded, and got, approval for the new locomotives to be streamlined, but this posed a problem for Stanier and Coleman, as the 'Princess Coronation' design was too far advanced to be designed as a streamliner from scratch. Their only option, if they were to meet their deadline, was to design an aerodynamic casing for the locomotives. This posed a problem too, because the sheer size of the 'Princess Coronation' left little scope for sloping anything. The best that could be done was to add a smooth casing along the sides of the boiler down to the wheels. At the front, again, length limits meant that a raked nose like the LNER's 'A4s' was out of the question: Coleman opted to bring the sloping sides together with a rounded top that actually sloped almost ten feet to form a smooth, rounded nose.

The design has been criticised for looking like an upturned bath tub, but that is really very unfair. Comparing photographs of the streamlined 'Duchesses' with the LNER's *Mallard* at the National Railway Museum reveals just how different the designs were, in purpose as well as appearance. *Mallard* is much more delicate of line, like a lightweight sports car – built for speed more than power. *Duchess of Hamilton* is the opposite, all power and thrust – a muscle car rather than a racing car.

The streamlined casing was difficult to build, though, as Eric Manley, tasked with making the complex front doors, recalls:

> One of the problems was that if the doors weren't exactly right the wind would get behind them and blow them open – there was more than one case of them hitting bridges.
>
> The boiler makers came and bent the ¼-inch plate to the basic shape of the doors and we were doing the brackets, bending them by hand to the right shape and marking them off before the welder came in to spot-weld them.

Though it was later tried to justify the streamlining on economic grounds, the reality is that it was a commercial imperative rather than an operational one. There was no significant saving of coal consumed, and it made maintenance more difficult. As for its effect on performance, it was rather like the spoiler on a car, giving the appearance of speed but making absolutely no difference to how the car drives. Unlike a car spoiler, the streamlined casing weighed five tons, and if it hadn't been for Coleman's efforts at cutting weight to the minimum, the 'Princess Coronations' would have been way over the civil engineer's limit.

The new locomotive took shape rapidly, and in April 1937 was sufficiently advanced for the LMS press office to invite selected railway journalists to inspect it. The journalists were impressed, and the *Railway Gazette*, a trade magazine that later became *Railway Gazette International*, published a technical analysis of it. What the *Railway Gazette* showed was that underneath the streamlined casing was a highly advanced conventional steam locomotive that pushed British limits on size and weight as far as they could be.

The first locomotive, No. 6220 *Coronation*, was completed at Crewe on 1 June 1937. She emerged painted in a light-blue livery with stripes converging on the front of her nose. She was certainly a contrast to the 'Princess Royals', which were all maroon, and the LMS lost no time in raising publicity, with a series of events, the most spectacular being on 13 June when she was filmed on the four-track line between Llandudno Junction and Colwyn Bay alongside the 1911 Coronation train hauled by an ex-LNWR locomotive, and a replica Liverpool and Manchester Railway train hauled by the world's oldest working steam locomotive, *Lion* of 1837. The coverage received was good, but could *Coronation* live up to expectations – and would the special new train she would haul match the art-deco glamour of the LNER's streamliners?

Chapter Five
'Coronation Scot'

Part of the answer came on 29 June 1937, when a special press trip from London to Crewe was arranged. Unlike the LNER, which had always been somewhat coy about its speed record attempts, there was little doubt amongst the assembled journalists that the LMS was going to have a crack at the LNER's record of 112mph, set by *Silver Link* in 1935.

A kitchen car was left out of the train, bringing the weight down to 263 tons, and *Coronation* was now well and truly run in. The only problem the LMS had was that its main line wasn't really suitable for very high speeds. For running fast on rails, the track needs to be straight and level – or, if a speed record is being attempted, downhill. The West Coast Main Line has plenty of steep gradients on which very high speeds could be reached, but all are hampered by curves or stations nearby, rendering them useless. The LNER, by contrast, had the 1-in-178 to 1-in-200 Stoke Bank, between Grantham and Peterborough, to race down, with little to force trains to slow until the little station of Essendine, some eleven miles south.

The best the LMS could manage was the descent from Whitmore summit northwards towards Crewe. It starts at 1-in-348 for 1¾ miles, followed by 1-in-177 for 3¼ miles, and then 1-in-269 for 2¾ miles, at the end of which the train is just under 1¾ miles from Crewe station and all the associated speed restrictions. At this point, even with an emergency brake application, it would be touch-and-go as to whether the train could stop safely in time.

The well-known train timer Cecil Allen wrote about the run in *British Pacific Locomotives*: 'The special had been scheduled to run to the "Coronation Scot" point-to-point timings, and nothing out of the ordinary was to be attempted until after Stafford. Nevertheless, we made a fairly exciting start to Tring, passing Willesden at 68mph, accelerating to 82mph up the 1-in-339 to Carpender's Park, and to 86.5mph at Watford.'

Clearing Willesden in just under eight minutes and Tring (31.65 miles) in 27 mins 45 secs was good going, but the maximum speed was only 87½mph: *Coronation* had a long way to go to beat the LNER. By Stafford, the train was five minutes ahead of the 114-minute schedule, but was restricted to just 30mph through the station. It wasn't until Norton Bridge, some 5½ miles away, that *Coronation* began to show what she could do. Presumably the fireman had been using the calm before the impending storm to build up a really big fire.

Speed increased to 85mph at Whitmore summit, the fireman ceaselessly working to keep pace with the boiler's insatiable demand for coal. Stanier's personal assistant (a man who would go on to great things later in his career) was Robert Riddles, who picks up Allen's story.

'We had decided not to pick up water at Whitmore to avoid reducing speed. The exhaust was humming with a continuous roar like that of an aeroplane engine. The white mileposts flashed past and the speedometer needle shot up through the "90s" and into the "100s" to 100, 111, 112, 113, 114 miles an hour.'

Coronation was absolutely flying and still had plenty left, but by this time, track was running out. 'Basford Hall sidings – 1½ miles away now; spectators from Crewe coming into view along the lineside, and the train still hurtling along at 114mph,' recalled Riddles.

'On went the brakes, off the regulator, but on we sailed, with flames streaming from the tortured brake blocks. The signals for Platform 3 at Crewe, entered by a reverse curve with a 20mph speed restriction, came into sight. We were still doing 60 to 70mph when we spotted the platform signal. The crockery in the dining car crashed. Down we came to 52mph through the curve, with the engine riding like the great lady she is. There wasn't a thing we could do but hold on and let her take it.'

It takes a lot to unnerve experienced railwaymen, but most on board were seriously rattled by now: speed was still far too high coming into Crewe, and as *Coronation* and her train approached the reverse curves at over twice the speed limit, they feared the worst – a high-speed derailment right into one of the most important railway stations in Britain. Even Stanier, normally so imperturbable, was reputed to have said, 'Now we're for it!' Allen, who had been on all the LNER's speed runs, was concerned – and so must have been the people watching from the station. For a brief moment, it looked almost certain that a good part of Crewe station would be annihilated by this train derailing.

Against the odds, *Coronation* and her coaches kept to the

rails, tribute to Stanier's suspension design on locomotive and stock. The deciding factor between success and disaster, though, was the quality of the track, which resisted the tremendous sideways force being exerted on it as the train passed through the reverse curves and into the platforms. Speed finally came down, and the train arrived in Platform 3 in just 6 min 58 sec – a minute less than the most optimistic estimates of eight minutes.

Shaken and distinctly stirred, the press corps got off the train. Official timings put the speed at 112mph, the same as *Silver Link*, but the speedometer in the locomotive said 114mph, and that was the figure that entered the record books. *Coronation* had become the fastest steam locomotive in the world. Ernest Lemon, by now a Vice-President of the LMS, offered some reassurance to the press. 'Of course, gentlemen,' he said, 'you will realise that we shan't need to do this kind of thing on every trip of the "Coronation Scot"; we were coming in a little faster than we shall have to in the ordinary course.' The relief was almost tangible.

A different perspective is provided by Frank Norris, the dining car attendant on the run, published in *Steam Railway* in 1980:

There was a tense excitement in the air at Euston. As the shimmering streamlined 'Pacific', 6220 *Coronation*, with her rake of eight coaches, prepared to leave, the bright daylight reflecting off her newly painted livery of blue with silver horizontal bands. I was already on board in my capacity as dining car attendant. The platform was crowded. Reporters were everywhere. Dozens of amateur photographers were busy taking pictures from all angles . . . everyone knew something really big was on.

As the guard gave the 'off', a loud cheer came from the platform. We had begun our journey.

By the time the train reached Bletchley, we were travelling at quite a steady speed, roughly about the 85mph mark. Through the dining car window, I noticed a plane was following us, towards the right-hand side of the coaches.

So far, it was a pleasant trip. The train ran smoothly on the metals. As the journey progressed, and I had served some of the travellers, I noticed that the scenery outside the window was moving much faster than normal.

I asked one of the journalists returning from the dynamometer car what our present speed was. To my surprise he said we had now reached 108mph and that an attempt on the speed record would be made soon after Whitmore.

Close to Stafford, I was serving coffee and drinks down the train. Going back to the kitchen car several times replenishing my serving tray, I had barely noticed the progress of our journey. I was halfway down the train again when we thundered through Whitmore.

Instantly I knew we were at the summit. By the other side of Madeley, we were really travelling. Smoke from the engine engulfed the train. Soon after passing Betley Road, we gathered more speed. In no time I realised from the surrounding scenery that we were only about two miles from Crewe.

Suddenly I felt the brakes being applied. We were now on the crossovers leading in. The whole train shuddered and gave a nasty lurch to one side: how it held the rails, I do not know. Any moment I thought it would foul the points as we passed under the large signal gantry.

It was impossible to hold the pot of coffee I was carrying, and it fell with a crash to the corridor floor. Luckily we made it to Crewe intact, thanks to the excellent driving of Tom Clarke.

On my return to the dining car I found the other attendants had been less fortunate. Cutlery and plates had slid off the tables, lying everywhere. Some half-empty coffee cups had been spilled over, staining the white cloths. Glasses and crockery had been smashed in the pantry due to some of the small sliding cupboard doors being left open. One unlucky traveller had even received a silver dish full of hot vegetables over him. With apologies from the attendant and a clean down, all was taken in good part.

Almost as good was to come on the return run, for which the operating authorities had generously given a time of 135 minutes. Driver Clarke had a free hand and went for it in one of the fastest runs ever recorded in steam-age Britain. He knocked 16 minutes off the schedule, arriving in Euston in 119 minutes, at an *average* speed of 79.7mph throughout. Of these, 150 miles were at an average of 83.2mph, and 72 miles at 88.9mph. *Coronation* hit 100mph again, this time at Castlethorpe, north of Wolverton, and came within a whisker at Kings Langley. These were timings that wouldn't look out of place in today's timetable: the 0713 from Crewe runs non-stop to Euston today in 108 minutes, on a 125mph, electrified line with tilting trains.

Although most in the know never really gave the 114mph figure credence, that was the number that appeared on the front page of the *Daily Sketch* on 30 June. '114mph by rail!' screamed the headline, with a head-on shot of *Coronation* in full cry next to it. 'Left Euston at 9.50am,' said one boxed item on the page, with another giving arrival and departure times from Crewe, and final arrival at Euston. There was a picture of Driver Tom Clarke and Fireman John Lewis being congratulated by Crewe's stationmaster, and of them meeting Ernest Lemon with locomotive inspector S. Miller. It's not often railways hit the front page of newspapers with such positive coverage, but this was one such occasion, and it was well deserved.

An interesting side effect of the streamlining on the 'Duchesses' was that it appears to have acted as something of a noise chamber, amplifying the noise made by its thin steel sheeting. It seems likely that *Coronation*'s thundering exhaust beat was complemented by a loud 'thrumming' as on her high-speed run: what a spectacle that would have been!

The next step, of course, was to get the 'Coronation Scot' running, and it must be said that the schedule wasn't nearly as ambitious as it could have been now that the new locomotive's speed credentials had been proven. It would depart from London and Glasgow at 1330, with a two-minute stop at Carlisle for a crew change. Arrival in both cities was at 2000 – six-and-a-half hours was easily achievable, and really should have been less. Still, it was a massive improvement on the 8¼ hours to which an agreement signed between the West and East Coast companies had limited journey times all the way from 1896 to 1932.

But to say that just because the LMS could have operated the 'Coronation Scot' faster it should have is to miss the point. The train was designed as a response to the LNER's streamliners, so its purpose was more to act as a flagship for the LMS than be a money-maker. It was commissioned in haste, but for once, the traditions of the company's constituents were a blessing rather than a curse. The LNWR and the Midland had both prided themselves on the standard of their carriages and the LMS continued this. Unlike the LNER, which had to design a new train from scratch, so good were the riding qualities and noise levels of the LMS carriages that vehicles could be more or less taken off the production line and fitted with the snazzy new interior that made these streamlined trains so glamorous.

Twenty-seven carriages were built or converted, and organised in three sets of nine. The formation was simple: first brake, first, first diner, kitchen car, two third diners, kitchen car, third diner and third brake. Just six were built new, the rest being taken from fleet stock and thoroughly upgraded.

By today's standards, it was a bizarre formation, with the focus very firmly on catering (which perhaps isn't that surprising given the journey time). The two brake coaches had large luggage compartments in the rear third so that passengers could repose without the encumbrance of suitcases and so on. But the use of two kitchen cars and two brake coaches meant that seating was surprisingly restricted: just 82 first-class and 150 third class passengers could be accommodated. By contrast, a first class coach on one of Virgin's Pendolino trains can seat 37 in comfort, and a standard class (today's equivalent of third class) 76, so five Pendolino coaches could accommodate almost as many people as the nine-coach 'Coronation Scot' did in 1937 (with one acting as a kitchen car). It must be said, though, that although the journey would be faster, it probably wouldn't be any more comfortable.

Inside the coaches of the 'Coronation Scot' was wood panelling from parts of the British Empire, and, in one of the third class coaches, from wooden piles from underneath the then recently dismantled Waterloo Bridge. Wilton carpeting was fitted throughout, and overall, the coaches were an improvement on even the best of the rest of the LMS's fleet.

The finishing touch was a blue and silver paint scheme to match *Coronation*, and when viewed from the side the complete ensemble looked spectacular. *Coronation*'s almost bullet-like nose made the train look smooth and sinuous, with no abrupt straight edges to jar the eye. The publicity department did its work, and all was set in motion for the service's debut on 5 July 1937.

That lunchtime, crowds lined the platforms of Euston and Glasgow Central to watch the trains depart – people were much prouder of the country then, and this sort of event was a kind of theatre that everyone could see and take pride in. This was, after all, the LMS's response to the gauntlet laid down by the LNER. It was a statement of intent and of capability, and the effect on morale of LMS staff and on people who lived near the route must have been significant: this train showed that whatever those redoubtable folk on the East Coast Main Line could do, the West Coast could do as well or perhaps even better. The trains ran to time (as one would expect), with *Coronation* hauling the northbound train and No. 6221 *Queen Elizabeth* hauling the southbound equivalent. All in all, the launch was a success.

Ironically, though, it was one of the few times when the two great rivals might have been better swapping timetables, because although the 'Coronation Scot' linked the two great cities in Britain, London and Glasgow, the timings were those of a train aimed at leisure travellers rather than the businessmen who formed the train's natural market. By contrast, the LNER served Edinburgh, which back then was far more a tourist destination than a business or political one, at times calculated for businessmen!

The 'Coronation Scot' ran five days a week, and proved extremely punctual, but it wasn't as spectacular an operation as the LNER's streamliners. While *Coronation* and her sisters had plenty in hand, the LNER's streamliners ran much closer to the limits of practical railway operation, so there were no surprises as to which the enthusiasts and train timers of the day were drawn to.

The first batch of 'Princess Coronations' was built in 1937, and there were five of them. Following No. 6220 *Coronation* were No. 6221 *Queen Elizabeth*, No. 6222 *Queen Mary*, No. 6223 *Princess Alice* and No. 6224 *Princess Alexandra*. In between the launch of the 'Coronation Scot' in July and October that year, they had proved extremely successful – after the faltering steps taken with the 'Princesses', Stanier and his team had now demonstrated their mastery of the art of steam locomotive design. It meant that in October that year, when the Chief Operating Officer and Stanier requested another ten locomotives, the Mechanical and

Electrical Engineering Committee approved, and backed the reconstruction of a bridge between Handforth and Cheadle Hulme on the Crewe–Manchester line to allow the new locomotives to run at line speed. All were named after duchesses, and it wouldn't take long for this prefix to become the popular nickname for the entire fleet.

This time, though, the operating department got its way. Although the first five would be streamlined, the second half of the order would not. This reflected sound operating pragmatism. As glamorous as the streamlined locomotives were, they weren't the easiest on which to conduct routine maintenance and servicing. Those sloped sides prevented the usual walkway (known as a running plate) being installed, so to get access to sanders and lubricators, maintenance staff and engine crews had to use ladders. Similarly, the huge nose doors had to be opened outwards in order to gain access to the smokebox. Although flaps and access ports were installed to make life as easy as possible, the simple fact was and is that on a steam locomotive streamlining makes maintenance more difficult.

When No. 6230 *Duchess of Buccleuch* emerged from Crewe on 27 June 1938, the public got its first sight of what Coleman and his team had in mind when they first penned *Coronation*. The streamlined casing had gone, and now the giant boiler, smokebox snugly fitted above the cylinders, high running plate and imposing profile could be seen. It was quite a contrast, but the unstreamlined locomotives were if anything more elegant than their metal-clad counterparts. Here was a design of contrasts: of power and poise, of brute strength yet blessed with considerable intelligence of design.

And above all, they looked bigger and stronger than anything else on the rails. They were magnificent.

Of course, with unstreamlined locomotives in service, there was a rush to prove or disprove whether the fuel savings gained by streamlining outweighed the difficulty of maintenance and operation. A study by Derby claimed that despite there being little if anything in it in terms of coal consumption, the figures it produced predicted a saving in coal of between 7.7 and 12.79 tons in every four-week period for the streamlined engines – up to 150 tons a year. However, another set of figures based on records from coaling plants suggested the opposite. Derby said their records were inaccurate, and that the streamlined tenders allowed more coal to be spilled than their conventional counterparts. Derby then claimed it all proved consumption was equal – why, is lost in the mists of time. The reality is that at the speeds required of the 'Duchesses', whether streamlined or not, far greater wind resistance came from the sides of the train than the front. Smoothing the undersides of the carriages with skirts almost down to rail level could well have made as much difference.

You'd have thought at this point that the arguments for and against streamlining would have been won decisively by the conventional locomotives – but once an organisation gets a taste for glamour, it's very difficult to give it up, so the next batch of locomotives, this time twenty-strong, was all to be streamlined. Construction was scheduled for 1939.

Chapter Six
Power to the People

By the start of 1939, there were enough 'Duchesses' in service and in the pipeline for the operating department to start seriously considering how best to use these powerful and fast locomotives.

Most duties didn't demand anything like their power, and were undertaken by smaller locomotives, such as the 'Royal Scots', 'Patriots' and 'Jubilees'. Although the 'Duchesses' could and did run on the heavier trains from Euston, these were still timed for the smaller locomotives: there simply weren't enough of the big 'Pacifics' around to guarantee one would be available. Nonetheless, the operating department wanted to see just how much the locomotives could haul while still meeting the timetable. After all, it made sense to use them on duties nothing else could match and leave the lighter loads for smaller engines. It seems there was an aspiration to use the 'Duchesses' – assuming they really were as powerful as they should be – to haul ultra-heavy passenger trains on the demanding line from Crewe to Glasgow.

The concept was that where two trains ran to Glasgow, say one from Birmingham and another from London, rather than both carrying on with their own locomotives, the carriages from both would be coupled together at Crewe to form one massive twenty-coach train for the leg to Glasgow. Operationally, it made a great deal of sense as it meant that just three locomotives rather than four would be needed, and it would save a crew as well. By running one train north of Crewe rather than two, space on the track could be saved, which could be used by other trains. But if this was to be anything other than a dream concocted by the operating department, the 'Duchesses' needed to prove their power.

The locomotive chosen for the tests was No. 6234 *Duchess of Abercorn*. She was built in August 1938, without stream-lining, and the test was planned for 12 February 1939 (a Sunday, when fewer trains ran). Anticipation at Crewe was high as the locomotive backed onto her twenty-coach train – a load of around 600 tons to haul to Glasgow.

The crew faced a major challenge getting this train moving at any sort of speed at all, and so it proved. *Duchess of Abercorn* struggled, losing five minutes on the scheduled time by Warrington, just 24 miles north. By Carnforth, she had dropped a shade over ten minutes and still faced the stiff climb to Shap, some 31½ miles away. The test car behind the locomotive recorded what was going on. By Oxenholme, just under thirteen miles north of Carnforth, the deficit was running at around fifteen minutes, and the maximum power recorded at the drawbar – the coupling between the locomotive and the train – was 1,348. By Tebay, thirteen miles further on, power had risen to 1,720hp, and a couple of minutes had been recovered. By Shap summit the train was running 12½ minutes late, and *Duchess of Abercorn*'s power output was diminishing. Arrival at Carlisle was ten minutes late.

From there, things continued. The official report was withering: 'Between Carlisle and Beattock [39.7 miles away]

9.4 minutes were lost by the engine, mainly due to the indifferent steaming of the engine, the management of the fire not being up to the required standard.'

This was damning stuff – either the engine crews weren't making enough effort to meet the schedule, or the 'Duchesses' simply weren't up to the job. What was particularly disappointing was the maximum drawbar horse-power. Although 1,935hp recorded at Calthwaite on the southbound run wasn't bad, *Duchess of Abercorn* should have been able to do this for rather longer – if the operating department hadn't thought so it wouldn't have suggested the trial in the first place.

The engineering team wasn't overly put out by this as it thought a simple modification would transform the loco-motive, and you can try a simple experiment at home to see what they did. When the cylinders have finished with the steam, it is sent out through an exhaust pipe and into a nozzle under the chimney called the blastpipe. The 'chuff chuff' sound steam locomotives make is the exhaust from the cylinders leaving the blastpipe and then travelling upwards through the smokebox and through the chimney.

Getting the diameter of the blastpipe right is crucial. If it's too small, not enough steam can escape from the cylinders, strangling performance, while if it's too big, the steam escapes too quickly, and that's a problem too as the steam passing through the blastpipe and chimney sucks gases from the firebox through on its way out but in short, soft gasps rather than the near-continuous pull that brings the best results.

To illustrate this, you'll need a jug of hot water that's

letting off plenty of steam (being careful not to scald yourself), two straws and a tube like that from a kitchen roll. Take a straw and blow through it as hard as you can. The air from the straw moves the steam, and takes some with it, quickly being replaced from around the jug and with steam from the hot water. If you've blown as hard as you can through the straw, you'll have found that you can't get enough air through it, and the pressure builds up in your cheeks. This is similar to what happens when a locomotive blastpipe is too narrow.

Now try with the large tube. This time, you can get a lot of air through it, but unless you're blessed with the lungs of a tenor, you'll quickly run out of puff, and this is what happens when the blastpipe is too large – you can get a lot of air moving, but very quickly run out of breath, meaning that you have to recover before you can do it again. On a steam locomotive this means that you get short, soft blasts of draught on the fire, which limits the amount of air going through it, and thus the steaming rate.

But if you try with both straws together, you get a happy medium – you can sustain a puff for a good while, while not stretching your cheeks with back-pressure. And there's an added benefit too: because the air coming from two straws has twice the surface area, it picks up even more steam with it than if you simply have one tube twice the area of the straw. It gives a better pull of air through the firebox, carries more gases with it and doesn't put back-pressure on the cylinders. This is what the LMS did with *Duchess of Abercorn* – fitted a double-blastpipe and chimney to make the fire burn hotter. The double-chimney, encased in an elegant oval wrapping, if anything made *Duchess of Abercorn* look even more powerful.

On 26 February, she set off on a repeat run, the crew determined to show what she could do. Driver Garrett and Fireman Farringdon from Crewe North shed would take *Duchess of Abercorn* to Carlisle, where a crew from Polmadie shed in Glasgow would take over for the run into Scotland. A different crew would return her to Carlisle, from where Garrett and Farringdon would return *Duchess of Abercorn* to her base.

Things didn't start off well, with a severe speed restriction at Winsford Junction, near Crewe. From there, where the timings started, things went better, with the train, which weighed 607 tons gross, passing Warrington on time (the schedule was the same as that for the 12 February run), and by Wigan, more than a minute and a half had been gained. The 12.8 miles from Wigan to Preston was covered in 16 min 55 secs, an average speed of just over 45mph, and she was still running almost two minutes ahead of time.

From Preston, things are fairly level on the twenty-seven miles approaching Carnforth, and if it hadn't been for a signal check on the approach to Lancaster, in all probability she would have passed bang on time, rather than the thirty seconds late that she was. There was no question that Garrett and Farringdon were well in charge of their steed, but now the going got tough.

From Carnforth to Oxenholme, thirteen miles away, the West Coast Main Line starts seriously climbing. First is a vicious 1-in-134 sprint for around 2⅓ miles followed by just over three miles of slightly downhill or level track. This gave the crew a chance to test their engine and see whether she was up to climbing, and then get the fire really hot and the boiler full for the first test – the climb up Grayrigg. Farringdon shovelled furiously, paying special attention to filling the back corners of *Duchess of Abercorn*'s giant firebox. By Oxenholme, up a gradient as steep as 1-in-111 in places, they'd gained two minutes, and the test coach had recorded a drawbar horsepower of 2,120.

Through Oxenholme she raced, despite the continuing steep climb, and after passing Grayrigg summit, Farringdon got the injectors on to fill the boiler for the stiffest test so far – Shap. *Duchess of Abercorn* passed Tebay, 95.4 miles north of Winsford Junction, in a time of 96 min 50 secs, gaining more than three minutes. Peak power dropped slightly, reflecting the water put in the boiler and coal in the firebox, which both cooled the engine briefly, and then *Duchess of Abercorn* demonstrated the sheer power and capacity of the design, haring up Shap with a load twice that of the 'Coronation Scot' in just over seven minutes on a leg scheduled for nine. It was then downhill to Carlisle, reached in 132 minutes from Winsford Junction, against 139 scheduled.

It was a great run, and Polmadie's Driver Marshall and Fireman Lynn continued it. The climb north from Carlisle to Beattock summit is one of the most demanding on Britain's railways, but Marshall and Lynn made a brilliant attack on it, passing the lonely station at Beattock, which marks the start of the serious climbing, in 39 min 40 secs, for a distance of 39.7 miles. The highest speed recorded was 80mph – and with a load that heavy, it was a great achievement. Beattock summit was reached almost four minutes ahead of time. From there, almost four minutes was dropped by Carstairs, but a good run to Glasgow Central saw the train arrive within thirty seconds of time.

Just two hours were given to turn *Duchess of Abercorn* round, refresh her coal and water, clean the fire of any clinker and check that all was well mechanically. The crew to Carlisle was a different one, Driver McLean and Fireman Smith, but they were of the same mould as the other crews that day and wasted no time in showing what a fresh pair of bodies could do. Between Motherwell and Law Junction, the flattest gradient is 1-in-137, with much of it at 1-in-103. An average speed of 46.7mph was little short of astonishing given the load.

They hammered Beattock into submission, and although it isn't as viciously steep as in the northbound direction, it is much longer. At the summit, a minimum speed up the final two miles or so of 1-in-99 of 62mph was the reward.

Carlisle was reached early – 9 min 30 sec early – and then Garrett and Farringdon took over once more. From Carlisle south, the line climbs all the way to Shap, thirty-one miles away, so high speeds take some time to build up. Nonetheless, by Wreay, 4.9 miles south of Carlisle, *Duchess of Abercorn* was already running at 42mph, and the next six minutes were to produce something extraordinary.

What Garrett and Farringdon did between Wreay and Calthwaite, six miles away, was to exploit the steam locomotive's characteristics to the full. It is possible for short periods, providing the crew know exactly what they are doing, for a steam locomotive to generate power way beyond what would normally be expected. What happens is this: normally, the fireman – who has to manage the boiler as well as shovel coal – tries to ensure that he fills the boiler at the same rate that water is being boiled. But adding cold water to the boiler cools the water already there down slightly, limiting the amount of steam that can be boiled. By stopping the injectors from filling the boiler and by ensuring the fire is white-hot over the whole grate, the water that's in the boiler boils at the fastest possible rate, generating more steam. It's the steam locomotive equivalent of a fighter jet igniting its afterburner: it uses a lot of fuel (and in this case water), and it can't be done for long as the boiler water would be consumed, but it delivers spectacular results if used in the right way.

Duchess of Abercorn was well able to take all the steam the boiler could generate, and so it proved. The climb to Calthwaite was stormed – no other word suffices – and speed rose to 64mph. It must have been an almighty spectacle – it was as if *Duchess of Abercorn* was charging forward in fury and defiance at the treatment being meted out to her. In the test car, the instruments showed just how hard this locomotive was working with her 607-ton load: 2,511 horsepower at the drawbar was recorded, and still speed continued to rise, passing Plumpton, 2.4 miles on, at 71mph. Power had fallen slightly on this level stretch, but was still sky high, at 2,394. At Penrith, *Duchess of Abercorn*'s speed peaked at 73mph, power at over 2,300hp, and if it wasn't for sharp curves forcing a slowing to 53mph from there, could have continued to rise.

What Garrett and Farringdon thought at this point isn't known, but they must have had a good idea they had well and

truly nailed the challenge laid down by the operating department as they slowed down and arrived in Crewe exactly to
the scheduled time. When you set such an outstanding
record, as these men did, there's no need to showboat.

When the figures were analysed, they proved little short
of astonishing. The modifications to *Duchess of Abercorn* had
transformed her. At Calthwaite, the best Garrett and
Farringdon had been able to get out of her was 1,935hp on
the 12 February run. Two weeks later, they'd improved on
that by hitting 2,511hp: an improvement of around 20%,
and an all-time British power record for a steam locomotive.
Furthermore, this wasn't a fluke – although 2,511hp was the
peak, levels at or around 2,000hp were maintained for long
distances on north and southbound runs, suggesting that the
real limitation now wasn't the engine: it was the fireman.

The achievement of the crews and of *Duchess of Abercorn* is
amplified when you consider that these power levels were
recorded at the coupling between the locomotive and train:
2,511hp was what was available to haul the train after the
locomotive had moved itself. In *British Pacific Locomotives*,
Cecil J. Allen calculated what the likely power outputs on
Duchess of Abercorn were, and the results are as impressive as
everything else about the run. The maximum horsepower
recorded by the locomotive was 3,333hp, and 3,000hp was
achieved at at least four other points for sustained periods.

In 1938, the LNER 'A4' *Mallard* set a world speed record
for steam of 126mph, and the achievements of Driver
Duddington and Fireman Bray – along with the locomotive's
designer, Sir Nigel Gresley – have entered railway folklore.
Yet, if one was being sceptical, you could argue that the per-

formance was exactly what one would expect: a powerful passenger locomotive should be able to go fast downhill. What Garrett and Farringdon, Marshall and Lynn, and McLean and Smith did was far more demanding, both physically and technically.

For the fireman, the challenge was simply to try to keep pace with *Duchess of Abercorn*'s appetite for coal – she had a big grate that needed to be covered in just enough coal to burn really hot (at a temperature of hundreds of degrees Celsius) but not so thin that parts of the grate would be uncovered by the time the fireman next got round to it. Although the driver didn't have as much physical work to do (though it would be surprising if the driver hadn't lent the fireman a hand on these runs), he had to use the minimum amount of steam possible in order for the fireman to keep pace. If he'd set the cut-off – the steam locomotive equivalent of a car's gear – too high, letting more steam into the cylinders, on *Duchess of Abercorn*, even with the best fireman in the company, it would have been desperately easy to drain the boiler of steam. It was a balancing act that they got absolutely right.

To place this in context, it took a long time for *Duchess of Abercorn*'s record to be beaten by anything comparable on British railways. We can exclude electric locomotives from this as they draw their power from overhead wires, meaning that they can be lighter and that more of the weight they have can be devoted to putting that power onto the rails: to compare them with *Duchess of Abercorn* would be unfair. But when you compare other 'prime mover' designs (i.e. anything that carries its own power source with it) with *Duchess of Abercorn*'s run, something very interesting happens. In terms of engine horsepower – the maximum a locomotive can generate – only three types of British diesel locomotive can claim to have engines as powerful as the 3,333hp maximum recorded by *Duchess of Abercorn*, and two of those are heavy freight designs. A few more have come close, but other than the 'Deltic' diesels of the early 1960s, in terms of engine horsepower, no passenger diesel locomotives have been able to put out quite as much. When you consider that the 'Deltics' operated on the East Coast Main Line, it wasn't until 1999 – sixty years later – when the 3,200hp Class 67 diesels entered service, that there was a prime mover passenger locomotive on the West Coast Main Line able to match the 'Duchesses' in terms of power output.

In the event, the long-term replacements for the 'Duchesses' were high-powered electric locomotives, making this comparison something of an academic exercise; nonetheless, it is a compelling thought that in 1939 there were steam locomotives in service capable of higher power than almost all of the products of the Modernisation Plan of the 1960s (of which more later).

Of course, no crew could have maintained *Duchess of Abercorn*'s performance for a whole journey, but this test run stands out as perhaps the most cogent demonstration of the design's power and potential. There was no doubt now about how good these locomotives were, but ironically the operating department never felt there was a need for the lengthy twenty-coach trains the 'Duchesses' had now demonstrated they could haul.

Chapter Seven
American Beauty

Nineteen thirty-nine was the year that the 'Coronation Scot' finally gained a bespoke set of carriages along the same lines as those used on the LNER's streamliners. Before they entered service, they were to represent Britain at the 1939 World's Fair, which was being held in New York. In a change from the blue and silver livery used on the first generation of stock, the new coaches were painted Crimson Lake with gold speed lines. Seven semi-articulated coaches, along with a first-class sleeping car, were sent over with the locomotive, No. 6220 *Coronation*, or at least that's what the intention was.

The powers-that-were decided not to send the first-built locomotive, preferring, instead, one of the latest batch. However, the uniform image presented by having *Coronation* present at the head of the 'Coronation Scot' was too compelling not to use, so they swapped identities with No. 6229 *Duchess of Hamilton* and sent the newer locomotive instead; I'll continue to refer to her real identity.

Duchess of Hamilton was the latest in a long line of British locomotives to visit North America, the most recent being the LMS's own No. 6100 *Royal Scot* in 1933 and the Great Western's No. 6000 *King George V* in 1927. The locomotive was fitted with the bell and electric headlight American operating requirements demanded, but the onboard safety equipment used on many American railways wasn't felt to be worth the expense, and this meant that *Duchess of Hamilton* would have little chance to stretch her legs. Crewe made sure she looked the part, even polishing her paintwork with beeswax to give it a rich lustre. She left the LMS from Euston to a cavalcade of flashes from photographers, and Stanier took the opportunity to inspect the locomotive one final time before she left Britain.

The train left in January 1939 from Southampton, arriving at Baltimore. It then undertook a lengthy tour to visit cities such as Baltimore, Washington, Philadelphia, Pittsburgh, Cincinnati, Louisville, Indianapolis, Chicago, Detroit, Cleveland, Buffalo, Albany, Boston, Hartford and many others – a distance of 3,121 miles, before arriving in New York on 14 April to take its place in the exhibition.

Robert Riddles (of *Coronation*'s speed run) was in charge of the train in North America, and in an address to the Junior Institution of Mechanical Engineers, gave a detailed account of the trip.

Unloading took place in temperatures which varied from 74F one day to 26F the next. Ice formed on everything. It was intensely cold, and the first major problem arose when the driver contracted pneumonia and was laid up for a month. I decided I would do the firing and let the fireman do the driving.

Our first day out with a trial run to Washington for press purposes started at 6am and finished at 2230. Unfortunately,

British and American locomotives are designed to burn widely different types of coal and that provided at Baltimore was, by our standards, little more than slack. We had to refill the tender at Washington, and I compute that on that day we burnt 11 or 12 tons of coal – or dirt! I admit to having done a little driving in lieu of firing.

It seems an odd thing to suggest that *Duchess of Hamilton* was suffering from having the wrong type of coal, but it was true. American locomotives had long gone beyond the capacity of a single fireman, and had mechanical stokers instead, which used very small coal as it flowed easily through the mechanism and onto the grate. The big problem with using small coal is that it burns more quickly than the heftier lumps used on British locomotives, and that meant more work for the fireman. But the coal also burned hotter, and the fittings inside *Duchess of Hamilton*'s firebox simply weren't designed to cope. It was the first of a series of problems Riddles and the crew had to deal with.

Touring under these conditions, even mechanical troubles were each a major headache. Our first trouble was a broken spring-bolt. This was made of manganese molybdenum steel, and there was nothing like it available locally, so we chose a valve spindle forging of similar tensile strength and turned it down to make a bolt.

At Harrisburg, our brick arch, of a new design, began to come adrift and as we had the Allegheny Mountains ahead of

us we had to put in one of the two spare arches which we
carried.

This stretch of line meant *Duchess of Hamilton* would have
to climb 1,055ft in 10.8 miles from Altoona to the 193ft
altitude of Gallitzin Tunnel, and a grade steepening from
1-in-58 to 1-in-40: a severe test for any locomotive, never
mind one that wasn't steaming well.

The work was so badly done that a third arch was necessary;
St Louis looked to be a big centre where labour should be
available, so I ordered the third arch to be ready there – but
what a hope! A boilermaker and his mate turned up to meet
us and offered themselves as the only ones available to do the
job. Meanwhile, three of the front rows of bricks of the arch
already fitted were found on our arrival at St Louis to have
fallen into the firebox, forming a fused mass. Although by
this time it was 1am, and we had to be away by 0900 the next
day, I had to insist on breaking up the fallen arch and getting
it out through the drop-grate – no easy task with bricks which
were white-hot and too large individually to be dropped
through the small opening without being broken down.

With the job done by 4.30am, I got to the hotel, where from
my appearance I should have been refused admission but for
the magic name 'Coronation Scot'. I had a bath and some
sleep, up at 8am to another bath, and off to the train to get
hold of the Mayor and open the exhibition. To allow the
engine to cool down we waited until 2pm before getting
busy, but there was still a pressure of 50psi in the boiler.
Only the boilermaker would go into the firebox, and there

were only the boilermaker, our own mechanic and myself to see the whole business through. In we went and suffice it to say that three hours heaving lumps of firebrick, some weighing 25lb and others up to 80lb (the whole arch weighs 17cwt), inside an engine firebox with 50lb pressure of steam all around you, is an experience not readily to be forgotten! However, the job was finished by 5pm, and an hour or so later the fire was in again and all was going well. Another bath, a rump steak and a bottle of champagne and bed.

By 9pm I was driving the train away to Springfield, some 120 miles distant, where we arrived at 1135pm for another bath and bed, after what might fairly be termed a busy day, but not without further incident. Anxious to get to our destination, running at 70 to 75mph, at a place called Plainview, up went a red flare, an American method of indicating an emergency sighted by running crews. On went the brake – regulator shut – and the train came to a stand some 200 to 300 yards from a motor-car that had missed its way and straddled the track. I drew the train up to the obstruction and getting down on the track met a very white-faced gentleman who told us he couldn't move. We got him back in his seat, and with our endeavours, together with his engine, in a smell of burning rubber as the tyres scraped on the ends of the rails, he shot forward into the night, and we went on, perhaps a little more soberly.

The reception given to *Duchess of Hamilton* was quite something, the Americans taking her to their hearts, and after leaving one station she departed at the same time as a streamlined diesel and a streamlined electric locomotive, and looked every bit as modern. Crowds lined the tracks and platforms to see her pass, and at Terre Haute, a Scots band was on the platform to welcome her. On arrival at New York, Riddles was met by the welcoming committee and heartily shook their hands: it had been a real adventure for all.

The journey across the United States provided an opportunity to compare the differences between American and British design. The most apparent was that of size, because, although *Duchess of Hamilton* was a giant by British standards, as far as the Americans were concerned, she was not much more than a medium-sized locomotive. Bridges and tunnels in America are much higher and wider than those in Britain, meaning the trains can be commensurately bigger and more powerful, which, given the huge distances across the country, means heavier loads can be carried further.

But there were differences too in design. Many American locomotives were designed for absolute ease of operation and maintenance. Parts that the crews needed to get to were made as accessible as possible, with the aim of allowing servicing and maintenance to be performed as quickly as possible, and with as few staff as possible. If that meant hanging things like pumps on the side of the boiler, or on the smokebox door, so be it: there was little scope in many designs for aesthetics. But not in all, and *Duchess of Hamilton* looked a good contemporary of the streamlined locomotives used in America. Yes, she was smaller, but in her smoothness of form she was a far more typical streamlined locomotive than her rival 'A4s' on the LNER.

The train's stay in America was extended by the outbreak of the Second World War. It was felt in the early days that the risk of it being sunk on the way back, as well as a shortage of shipping space, meant it wasn't worth trying to repatriate it. The train was moved to Jeffersonville, Indiana, where it was used as a living quarters for the U.S. Army Quartermaster Corps, while the locomotive went to Baltimore. She was repatriated in 1943, landing in Cardiff before running to Crewe where she swapped identities back to No. 6229 *Duchess of Hamilton* and resumed her career.

Chapter Eight
Last of the Line

When war broke out in 1939, it was the end of the line for the grand streamlined trains. The war effort came first, and that meant there was no room on the tracks for fast trains with limited capacity. Instructions were issued that all streamlined trains and their locomotives were to be stored for the duration. It was one of those directives that must have come from a civil servant who didn't know what a train was, as the locomotives on both the LMS and LNER were about the most powerful passenger designs in the country, and were far too important to be stored.

It didn't take long for the order for the locomotives to be stored to be rescinded, which was a good job as the LMS was still building 'Duchesses' at Crewe. It was quickly apparent that there would be labour shortages in many aspects of life as men and women were conscripted into the armed forces and to key industries such as mining and agriculture. At this point, one would have thought that all the locomotives being built would be outshopped as non-streamlined, but somebody in the LMS had other ideas, and Crewe continued to churn out streamlined 'Duchesses', with nine built between 1940 and 1943.

This was an odd decision, and it looks so still. We've already established that the streamlined 'Duchesses' were more difficult to service and operate than their conventional sisters, so when there was a national speed limit of 60mph imposed across the network, what possible advantage could be gained by streamlining? It could have been a question of prestige and pride, or perhaps even of propaganda – but it's difficult to believe that anyone would really have made a big issue of whether new steam locomotives were streamlined or not: there were far more important things on people's minds. Very quickly, all were painted black, a colour that looked particularly drab on the streamlined locomotives. It was a practical decision, both from the point of view of reducing their visibility from the air and also from that of painting – if all locomotives were black, the cost of the paint would be less too. Even so, it removed the last vestige of glamour from the railways: now all locomotives were workhorses rather than racehorses.

Stanier was busy in the first couple of years of the war altering parts of the LMS locomotive works for production of munitions, and in 1942 was seconded full-time to the Ministry of Production. His knowledge of where and how things could be made was to prove vital. Nonetheless, the 'Duchesses' continued to emerge from Crewe. In 1940, five were built, all streamlined, and in 1943 another four streamliners emerged from Crewe. It was at this point that the penny dropped and streamlining was abandoned for new locomotives. The following year, another four 'Duchesses' were built, before a brief hiatus in 1945.

And the war didn't stop Stanier considering the next developments in passenger locomotive design. At the top of the list was an express passenger locomotive that would have been even more powerful than the 'Duchesses'. With a 4-6-4 wheel arrangement (as compared with the 4-6-2 of the 'Duchesses') and a grate area of 70 square feet, it would have needed a mechanical stoker to keep the fire burning. The boiler pressure was 300psi, and overall tractive effort would have been 56,070lbs, compared with the 40,000lbs of the 'Duchesses'.

The war was a time of great change for the LMS and railways in general. The LMS lost Lord Stamp in an air raid in 1941, and Stanier himself retired in 1944, after reaching the very pinnacle of an engineering career and a year after being knighted. Despite his retirement, he would continue to enjoy an active interest in railways, and the respect of his peers. After retirement, he was elected to the Royal Society, such was the esteem in which he was held.

Stanier's successor was Charles Fairburn, and Fairburn continued Stanier's work, always seeking to improve designs and maximise efficiency. At this point, the war was gradually starting to be won, and Fairburn looked ahead to try to envisage what the LMS might need in the future. A number of things were clear: labour shortages would continue; traffic would remain heavy; and until the track was brought up to pre-war standards (maintenance was at the minimum safe level during the war) speeds would remain fairly low.

The import of American heavy freight locomotives proved a real eye-opener for British railways, as they had a number of labour-saving features that could easily be applied to locomotives here. They had hopper ashpans, which were hinged at the back and could be emptied by lifting a locking catch and lifting a lever. Most locomotives in Britain needed some poor soul to go underneath the locomotive in an ash pit and literally rake out the ash with rods. It's a horrendous job, and if there's any water in the bottom of the ash pit (which there often was) the hot ash, often with burning coals that had slipped through the grate, would flash the water to steam, choking the man raking out the ashpan.

They also had rocking grates, which made the other particularly unpleasant maintenance task easier. Rather than having a fixed grate in the firebox, a rocking grate was split into a number of panels, linked at the bottom by a rod that led to a lever in the cab. Rather than having to laboriously break up the fire with a long, pointed pole called a dart, and then having to use a long-handled shovel called a paddle to take the burning coals out of the firebox and throw them over the side, once any clinker had been broken, the rockers in the grate could be set to their vertical position, and the fire would fall through the gaps, through the (hopefully) open ashpan and into the pit. It saved hours in servicing time, and made working life much more pleasant for crews and maintenance staff. So impressed was the LMS by these simple modifications that over time it fitted all the 'Duchesses' with them.

Fairburn's reign wasn't to last long as he died in 1945 at the age of 58. His successor was yet another man from the Stanier mould, Henry Ivatt, the son of the celebrated Great Northern Railway CME of the same name. Ivatt was to instigate the last development of the 'Duchesses', before nationalisation in 1948. At this time, the rapid spread of diesel locomotives in the United States had been noticed in Britain, and, despite the cost and complexity of the new power source, Ivatt was keen to assess whether its claimed advantages of greater efficiency and availability would outweigh its higher cost compared with steam locomotives.

Things were tough on the railway, and Geoff Hillyard, who started his career in 1946 straight from school, paints an evocative picture of what it was like on Crewe North shed. As an engine cleaner, he and his colleagues were tasked with keeping the fleet as clean as they could, but staff shortages meant that he was soon firing on local trips.

'When an engine has just been brought onto the sheds after a journey the first job is to fill the tender with coal. The "Duchesses" hold 10 tons, and with the fire properly built up, another couple of tons are needed too. The engine has all the clinker cleaned out of the fire and most of the fire is dropped into the ashpan.'

Hillyard reckoned that the worst job was oiling the locomotives, which on the 'Princess Royals' was a particularly challenging task that had to be done over an inspection pit.

The man has to climb up to stand on the brake rods and then squeeze between all the coupling rods and check on the cork plugs which seal the oil in the bearings. Most of this time the fireman is afraid another engine might be sent down the line and move the one being oiled because he could be crushed by the big ends.

At the same time, he has a large oil can in one hand to top up the oil, and an oil lamp with burning wick in the other to see what he is doing. It is as precarious as walking a clothes line in the dark, and because you couldn't see if it was properly full, you had to continue until it started running down your overalls.

The 'Duchess' sheds of Camden, Crewe North, Carlisle and Polmadie (near Glasgow) were at the front line in providing the locomotives needed to operate trains on the West Coast Main Line, and were a crucial part in the operations of that line. Camden, and its outstation a little further up the line, always had more 'Duchesses' than anywhere else, but allocations did change, with some loco-motives moving between them depending on operational and maintenance requirements.

There aren't many original steam sheds left in their original use as they were either closed or converted to use by diesel and electric locomotives, but it is still possible to get an idea of what they were like at the Great Western Society in Didcot, and at Barrow Hill Roundhouse, Chesterfield. Of these, the Great Western Society probably comes closest to recreating the sense of a steam depot, as it has few diesels. Though both differ from the West Coast Main Line sheds in architecture and fittings, the essential elements are very similar. They are best appreciated on a wet, windy, cloudy day or a crisp winter morning – the sort of days when a steam locomotive might be the last thing you'd want to see.

At Didcot, you gain access via a subway from the station, and this acts as a neutral zone between the present day and long ago. The first thing that strikes you is the space required – the main-line depots were and are big sites, with a lot of tracks to store, service and maintain the locomotives. The second thing that invariably surprises people is just what dirty places they are – and Didcot is a paragon of cleanliness compared with many sheds in steam days.

Much of the track is covered in fine black ash, both from accidental spillages of ash from wheelbarrows and loco-motive smokeboxes, and also because in an environment like that, ash makes perfectly reasonable ballast for track that's only going to be used at very slow speeds. In occasional places there might be clinker dug out of fireboxes, piled in heaps next to where the locomotives stood, and perhaps little piles of ash itself. There are a few water columns to feed the engines, and a coaling stage (a tower where wagons full of coal are tipped from a height into tenders and bunkers).

But it's the locomotives, of course, that make an engine shed. At Didcot, they're all Great Western engines, but the scene at Camden or Crewe North would have been eerily similar. At rest, steam locomotives can be rather like sleeping cattle, as their steam and hot water bubble and sizzle and spit out of drain cocks and injector pipes. As their boilers gradually cool down, parts of the locomotive con-tract with the cold, adding their own noises to the mix.

Early in the morning is the most atmospheric time, when the locomotives are being gradually warmed up. You can't just light a huge fire, get the water boiling and move off as that causes rapid heating and expansion of the boiler, setting up stresses that can easily cause expensive leaks. Far better to take your time, building up the fire bit by bit and letting the locomotive gradually wake up. In steam days, senior cleaners and old hands would light up the engines for the crews, as this was a process that could take many hours. In a big depot like Didcot, there would have been no moments of silence — somewhere would be the sound of a shovelful of coal being thrown into the firebox, or the injectors being put on to feed water into the boiler, or the coaling stage dropping its contents into a tender.

And when locomotives came off duty, the spectacle continued. After filling the tender or tank with water, and then ensuring the boiler was full, the crew moved their locomotive onto an ash pit so they could empty the smokebox full of char carried through the boiler tubes, and remove the ash and clinker from the firebox. With a 'Duchess' this was relatively easy, though the emphasis should be on the 'relatively'. They were fitted with rocking grates and hopper ashpans, and this made removing the fire nominally a more straightforward task. It didn't always work quite to plan, though. Sometimes a large lump of coal or clinker would jam the grate somewhere between horizontal and vertical, necessitating a lot of hammering with the dart, and often a fair amount of swearing, to either bash it through or to get it back above the grate for extraction with the paddle. Other times, parts of the grate could fall off. The firebars were attached to the rocking arms by two bits of metal, forming a triangle with the long, flat firebars forming the top. The hot environment of the firebox could loosen these, and if too many were missing, replacements had to be sought.

Only once the old fire had been cleaned of ash and clinker, and the basis of a new fire heaped at the back of the firebox to stop the locomotive from cooling too rapidly, could it be considered that the locomotive was safe to be moved onto a storage road, either by the steam left in the boiler or by a shunting locomotive, and left in the care of the depot staff.

In 1946, the last three conventional 'Duchesses', No. 6253 *City of St. Albans*, No. 6254 *City of Stoke-on-Trent* and No. 6255 *City of Hereford* were built. In 1947, the first of a pair of uprated 'Duchesses' was delivered. No. 6256 was named after her designer, and in a ceremony, Stanier unveiled the nameplates himself: *Sir William A. Stanier, F.R.S.* It was a fitting tribute to Stanier, and he must have been thoroughly delighted. But No. 6256 was rather different in some respects from her sisters. The aim was to raise the mileage between major overhauls from around 70,000 miles to 100,000. If successful, this would have had a major impact on the type's availability, and little expense was spared. Rather than plain bearings, No. 6256 was fitted with freer-running roller-bearings throughout, as well as manganese steel linings to the axleboxes and hornguides, which made them more resistant to wear. The trailing truck was redesigned to allow a rocking grate and hopper ashpan to be fitted, and the cab side sheets, which were extended down on most locomotives to visually match the bottom of the tender tank, were cut short at the actual cab floor. It also had much higher levels of superheating than the other 'Duchesses' in order to extract every last bit of power from the boiler.

While this was going on (and indeed, for a couple of years before) the streamlined 'Duchesses' were gradually having their streamlining removed. It followed a damning report from Ivatt, in 1945, that said the casings should be removed and replaced with smoke deflectors on either side of the smokebox. The first streamliner to be defrocked was No.

6235 *City of Birmingham*, and the other streamliners followed as they went into works. One peculiarity of this process was that the original smokebox was retained, including its sloping top. These were retained until they needed replacement as it made no difference to performance.

The reason was that, at the same time, the first of a pair of 1,600hp diesel locomotives was under construction at Derby Works. No. 10000 represented the cutting edge of technology and offered a glimpse into the future for passengers. On her own, she wasn't nearly as powerful as a 'Duchess', but working in tandem with a sister locomotive, 10001, which was being built alongside her, the pair would be. The comparison was to be a straight fight between the most advanced locomotives on the LMS, but, before it could even start, the railways were thrown into turmoil again by the nationalisation of the 'Big Four' and a handful of independents into a new leviathan: British Railways.

Chapter Nine
Giants Tested

The old certainties of the railways changed for ever on 1 January 1948 when British Railways was created. The private railway companies, having worked effectively under state control during the war, were never going to be given much chance of fighting nationalisation under the socialist government of Clement Attlee, and so it proved. For designers and draughtsmen across the country, it looked as if their jobs might be under threat as there was no question that British Railways would want to impose a new design philosophy on the country's railways. And it was a design philosophy based on the best traditions of Crewe.

British Railways' first CME was Robert Riddles, who during the war was credited with the economical 'Austerity' freight locomotives. These were basically disposable engines, built as cheaply as possible and with an expected life of just a few years. Nonetheless, the designs proved sound, and so Riddles was given the task of designing British Railways' first locomotives.

From nationalisation, British Railways had to decide what its new traction policy should be. In North America, steam was rapidly giving way to diesel traction, while in Europe, extensive plans for electrification were being developed by the likes of France and Germany. The advantages of these two forms of power over steam was that the locomotives could operate for longer periods between routine servicing, meaning fewer were needed, and the day-to-day cost per mile of operating them could also be less. Against that had to be set the much higher cost of diesel and electric locomotives, and, in the case of the latter, the installation of overhead wires or trackside third rails and associated sub-stations and equipment to power them.

Riddles and his team envisaged widespread electrification in the long term, with diesels gradually supplanting steam locomotives on non-electrified lines. In the short term, because steam locomotives were cheap to build and the support systems needed were in place, the decision was taken to design a new range of steam locomotives, the last generation in Britain. The intention was to replace elderly locomotives with modern equivalents that were more efficient, powerful and reliable. They were to have a design life of around thirty years, by which time it was hoped the electrification programme would be completed.

Before pen was even put to paper, however, it was decided to test the key express passenger, mixed-traffic and freight locomotives of the 'Big Four' companies against each other. The officially expressed aim was to compare and contrast design features and assess which of these would be desirable in British Railways locomotives. However, although some findings from the exchange would prove useful, this was as much a political exercise to reassure staff that their own equipment wasn't going to be sent straight to the scrapheap. Young trainspotters in the south, west, Midlands and east must have been bounding with excitement at the prospect of locomotives they might not ever have seen running on or near their home turf – and being able to underline the numbers in their Ian Allan 'ABC' spotter's books. The trials were known universally as the 'Locomotive Exchanges', and they were to throw up some surprising results.

The trials for express locomotives (there were others involving freight and general-purpose designs) had a wide-ranging cast. The oldest type in the exchanges was the Great Western's 'King', the first of which had entered service in 1927. Although they had a 4-6-0 wheel arrangement, these locomotives were almost as big as the 'Pacifics' on other railways, and they were the biggest locomotives of their configuration ever built in Britain. They had tremendous power and could run fast, but demanded expert crews to get the best out of them, and design features such as their inside valve gear had long been superseded by easier-to-access outside equivalents on other railways. Because the Great Western had greater clearances in bridges, tunnels and platforms than other railways, the 'Kings' were slightly wider than the other locomotives tested, and that meant they could only be used on the Great Western and East Coast main lines.

The next oldest was the streamlined 'A4' 'Pacific' from the LNER. Introduced in 1935, they were the fastest steam locomotives in the world, and epitomised the glamour of express rail travel in the 1930s. However, they weren't quite as powerful as some of the other designs, and their inside big ends had always been prone to failure.

Next in age terms came the 'Duchesses', and the loco-motive chosen was No. 46236 *City of Bradford* (all the LMS locomotives were renumbered with a '4' in front of their existing number at nationalisation), built in July 1939, and based at Camden. She was built as a streamliner, but had recently lost her casing in the interests of easier maintenance. The power of the locomotives was beyond doubt, and many confidently expected the 'Duchesses' to dominate the Locomotive Exchanges.

Next up, and the last of the big designs in the exchanges, was the Southern Railway's 'Merchant Navy' class. These were introduced from 1941 and were very different from the other locomotives, in appearance (they were encased in a slab-sided casing called 'air smoothing') and, crucially, in operation. The designer, Oliver Bulleid, had replaced conventional valve gear as seen on the 'Duchesses' with a chain-driven motion in a bid to reduce maintenance requirements. Nominally all that was required was for the oil bath that enclosed it to be topped up, but the chains tended to slacken and the oil bath to leak, making the most modern design of all a rather erratic performer, albeit one with a very free-steaming boiler.

Last was another LMS design, the 'Rebuilt Royal Scot'. Although based on the 'Royal Scot' 4-6-0s built from 1927, a comprehensive upgrade initiated by Stanier saw them fitted with new more efficient boilers and effectively transformed them into new locomotives. Though the smallest and least powerful locomotive of the five designs, the everyday performances of the 'Royal Scots' were out of all proportion to their size, which was why it was thought they provided a useful counterpoint to the big 'Pacifics' and the 'Kings' of the Great Western.

All were powerful and proven performers, and the

intention was to run them on key routes around the country to contrast performance. Coal and water consumption, reliability and timekeeping would all be tested over a short period and the results carefully scrutinised. For enthusiasts, it was also a chance to answer some important questions, albeit of a rather more subjective type: could a 'Duchess' go faster than an 'A4'? Would an 'A4' be equal to a 'Duchess' on the West Coast Main Line? Would, perhaps, the 'Royal Scot' outshine the 'King'? And what on earth would the relatively unknown 'Merchant Navy' be like?

All things considered, the 'Duchesses' should have won the trials, followed by the 'A4s' or 'Merchant Navys' in a close finish for second, then the 'Kings' and finally the smaller 'Royal Scots'. On the basis of in-service performance, this would seem a reasonable expectation.

The first set of trials took place on *City of Bradford*'s home turf, the West Coast Main Line between London Euston and Carlisle. This was the one place where the 'Duchess' could be confidently expected to leave the other locomotives in the shade, by virtue of her huge power and the detailed route knowledge of the crew. The speed restrictions on the route meant that any comparison with pre-war times was meaningless on most of the line, but on the steep section between Preston and Carlisle, all of the locomotives faced a severe test.

City of Bradford's crew tried to burn as little coal as possible in order to make their locomotive seem more efficient than the competition (which excluded the 'King' as it was too wide), and her performances weren't outstanding by comparison with her classmates. In this context, the fact that *City of Bradford* was only a couple of minutes shy of the fastest locomotive, 'Merchant Navy' 35017 *Belgian Marine*, is creditable, particularly given that all of the other locomotives were being driven much closer to their limits. However, the sheer number of speed restrictions and operating limitations placed on the three locomotives meant that it would be difficult to draw any conclusions about locomotive performance on *City of Bradford*'s home ground. Time, then, for a trip to the East Coast Main Line.

The next trials took place on the East Coast Main Line between King's Cross and Leeds – one of only two stretches of track where the 'King' could operate, as it was slightly wider than the other locomotives. On a preliminary run on 28 April 1948, *City of Bradford* ran from King's Cross to Peterborough 1 min 44 sec inside the 88-minute schedule, with a heavy load of 480 tons. It was a good start and suggested that the locomotive had plenty in hand and would get better as the crew got to know the route. However, it quickly became apparent that the crew were hell-bent on burning as little coal as possible, relying on making up time by racing downhill after letting the fire burn down on the up-grades. The result was that despite being considerably more powerful, *City of Bradford* was more than a minute slower than the much smaller 'Royal Scot' on tests between Leeds and Grantham. On occasions – when recovering from temporary speed restrictions, for example – *City of Bradford* was allowed to show what she could do, and showed a clean pair of heels to her competitors. But these were only brief flashes, and the unavoidable conclusion (if one took the results of this trial as gospel) was that the 'Duchesses' were rather sluggish machines.

On the first set of trials on the Western Region, between London Paddington and Taunton, *City of Bradford* hadn't impressed, and neither did she particularly on the Bristol-Newton Abbot leg of the Bristol-Plymouth trial, but between Newton Abbot and Plymouth lie the notorious Devon banks, a legacy of Brunel's failed atmospheric railway, and here, finally, *City of Bradford* performed as everyone knew she could. The first test, the 1-in-38 to 1-in-57 climb to Dainton, was crested at 27mph, the fastest of any locomotive in the trial. Between Newton Abbot and Rattery, 13 miles away, Driver Byford gained three minutes on the schedule with a time of 21 mins 55 secs. By Brent, 15.6 miles from Newton Abbot, *City of Bradford* was over a minute ahead of the other locomotives, and from there, Driver Byford was compelled to take things a little easier, arriving in Plymouth in 46 minutes, four ahead of schedule.

On the Southern Region, the line chosen was that from London Waterloo to Exeter, and after all the speed restrictions on the West Coast and East Coast Main Lines, here at last was a route virtually free from speed restrictions. The schedule from Waterloo to Salisbury, a distance of 83.8 miles, was 103 minutes, and for all the crews it was something of a challenge to hold their steeds back to avoid embarrassing the planners. However, things were different between Salisbury and Exeter, where a combination of stiff gradients, tight schedules and a number of stops meant the crews and engines had to be on top of their game.

Because there were no water troughs on the Southern

Region (water troughs were long troughs laid between the rails at strategic locations, from where steam locomotives could lower scoops from their tenders and replenish their supplies) *City of Bradford* was provided with a tender from a wartime freight locomotive that had greater water capacity.

City of Bradford's performances were exactly what observers had come to expect – slow uphill to save coal, and then explosive downhill. It was on one of the Exeter-Waterloo journeys that *City of Bradford* showed a little of what she could do after arriving at Templecombe 4.5 minutes late. She made the quickest start of all to Abbey Ford, and on the winding line to Wilton had her speedometer almost fixed between 75 and 82mph. Then the driver seemed to lose interest in gaining on the schedule, and it was back to her usual methods.

The frustrating thing was that during the week before trials started properly, on 17 June, *City of Bradford* showed exactly what she could do after being held by adverse signals near Andover. Driver Byford launched the locomotive from Andover, *averaging* 82.6mph on the 22.3 miles between Worting and Brookwood, a few miles short of Woking. *City of Bradford* screamed through Basingstoke at speeds well into the 80s and on the way into the 90s, before having to slow to 15mph on the approach to Woking. The top speed was 88mph, and despite losing thirteen minutes due to signal checks and speed restrictions, *City of Bradford* arrived in London Waterloo just seven seconds late. It was a great demonstration of the locomotive's power, but on the Southern Region she was never allowed by her driver to repeat it.

Although the trials weren't a waste of time, it must have been difficult for the authorities to make a meaningful comparison of the types. The GWR 'King' was too big to operate on most routes and had a number of outmoded design features, so it could hardly be considered as a candidate for replication, while the methods chosen by Driver Byford on *City of Bradford* meant that the 'Duchess' was seldom allowed to demonstrate her power. The Southern Railway's 'Merchant Navy' was a good steamer but heavy on coal, while the LNER's streamlined 'A4s' proved powerful and fast but prone to failure. On balance, the Locomotive Exchanges were of far more value to enthusiasts than to British Railways, at least in pure engineering terms.

Despite the results of the exchanges, the position of the 'Duchesses' at the top of Britain's passenger locomotive tree was secure until well into the 1950s. Other designs had their advocates – the 'A4s' were perhaps a shade faster and more economical, for example – but the fact was that, on a day-to-day basis, the 'Duchesses' were there or thereabouts when it came to factors such as efficiency, speed and reliability, and significantly ahead when it came to power. It was a vindication of Stanier and Coleman's terrific design.

Replacement of the 'Duchesses' and their contemporaries in other areas wasn't on the cards. It was felt that these designs would be able to hold the fort for a good while yet, and so Crewe, Camden, Polmadie and Carlisle retained their allocations and continued to use their locomotives on the heaviest passenger trains in the country.

However, one of the biggest problems faced by the London Midland Region, which encompassed most of the lines of the old LMS south of the Scottish border, was that, with only thirty-seven 'Duchesses' and eleven 'Princess Royal' 'Pacifics', there simply weren't enough of them to do the work out there. That was why in 1952 the decision was taken to convert the Turbomotive, the experimental turbine-driven version of the 'Princess Royal', which had been withdrawn from traffic in 1949, into a conventional locomotive.

Although she was nominally the third 'Princess Royal' when she emerged from Crewe Works, she was neither properly a 'Princess Royal' nor really a 'Duchess'. Her boiler was more like that of a 'Princess Royal' (which one would expect given that her original boiler would probably still have been sound) but the chassis was more like that of a 'Duchess'. The argument was that, given that the chassis had to be largely rebuilt anyway, it would be daft to perpetuate the complex inside motion of the 'Princess Royals' when the arrangement used in the 'Duchesses' was far better.

So *Princess Anne* entered service in the summer of 1952, but her career would be cut short by a horrific accident near London, the precise cause of which is still unknown today.

Chapter Ten
Tragedy at Harrow

October 8 1952 dawned chilly and misty, the sun trying and failing to burn through the morning fog – a typical autumn morning, but one on which the railway took no chances. In those days, when signals were mostly lit by oil lamps and were thus hard to see in heavy mist and fog, the railway took special measures to limit the risk of trains passing signals at danger. Speeds were limited and detonators – explosive caps placed on the rails that explode when the train runs over them – were placed on the approach to critical signals to warn drivers to slow down and make sure they were clear. It wasn't speedy railway operation, but it was safe railway operation.

Gradually the mist cleared and the railway resumed normal operation, trying to recover the inevitable delays that mounted up during foggy weather. One of the trains that had lost a lot of time was the overnight sleeper train from Perth, which had left at 2015 the night before. It had departed Crewe thirty-two minutes late, and had lost more time on its way south.

Its late running presented a dilemma for the signalmen at Harrow & Wealdstone, near London, at around 0815. The 0731 Tring to Euston was due to depart at around the same time the Perth train was now expected to arrive. The question was whether to delay the sleeper train further and let the Tring to Euston train depart ahead of it, or to delay the otherwise almost-on-time commuter train. The signalman decided, correctly, that a few more minutes' delay on the sleeper wouldn't matter now, and so he signalled the local train out and set the signals for the sleeper train at danger.

The local train was normally formed of seven coaches hauled behind a large tank engine, but today a pair of old timber-bodied coaches had been added to cope with demand. It would make little difference to punctuality, and was a good example of how the railway used to be able to add capacity fairly easily. Meanwhile, the London-bound sleeper train continued its journey south, passengers probably awake by now and looking forward to getting off the train. They didn't know that they had already passed two danger signals and were heading at high speed into Harrow when they should have been stood at a signal some miles further back along the line.

Just as the guard of the Tring to Euston train was about to blow his whistle for departure, he looked to the train's rear and froze. Coming towards his train, on his line, was the Perth to London sleeper train, headed by No. 46242 *City of Glasgow*. It shouldn't have been anywhere near his train – and it was going much too fast to stop. *City of Glasgow*'s crew finally woke up to the danger and slammed on the brakes, but it was too little, too late.

The disaster unfolded almost in slow motion. *City of Glasgow* smashed into the rear of the commuter train, shattering the back three coaches and punching a two-inch depression into the track. The 'Duchess', by now derailed and out of control, turned to her right and over the northbound fast line. In just a couple of seconds, Harrow station had turned into a horror station. People rushed to help the survivors, but an already dreadful situation was about to get even worse.

A few minutes earlier, before the accident had happened, the signalman had accepted the 0800 express to Liverpool and Manchester, led by No. 45637 *Windward Isles* and the newly converted No. 46202 *Princess Anne*. The locomotive crews would have been completely unaware there was anything amiss and, as there was no need to stop at Harrow, were haring along at around 60mph. As they approached, one can only imagine their reactions as they saw the wreckage settling from the collision between the sleeper train and commuter trains – wreckage that lay right in their path. They made a hasty emergency brake application, for sure, but beyond that there was nothing they could do other than to try to find a safe place to ride out whatever happened next.

Windward Isles hit *City of Glasgow* pretty much head on and such was her speed that she reared over the big 'Pacific', followed by *Princess Anne* behind. Onlookers and survivors from the first crash dived for cover, but for some, there was no chance as the two locomotives on the northbound express crashed through the station footbridge, its girders cruelly swatting victims out of the way. The momentum of *Windward Isles* carried her over the platform and onto the southbound electric line, but *Princess Anne* twisted onto her side, careering over the platform and finishing up with her cab and tender resting on it.

The first few coaches of the Liverpool and Manchester express were wrecked, and Harrow station looked as if it had been bombed. In just a couple of minutes, it had been turned from a bustling commuter station feeding London into a charnel house. 112 were killed and 150 injured, but even so it could have been much worse. Had the locomotives or carriages caught fire – or had an electric train not managed to stop just short of the station, the death toll would have been higher still.

Harrow & Wealdstone was one of the most horrific railway accidents in Britain of all time, because of the casualties, and the cruel way it unfolded. To this day nobody knows why the crew of *City of Glasgow* failed to slow down at not one, but two red signals. It's possible they could have fallen asleep, but these were experienced men who would have known the line and the procedures in fog well. It could be that some calamity on the footplate – and this is what the noted rail safety expert Stanley Hall thinks happened – disabled them or prevented them from reaching the brake handle, something like a fractured steam pipe, for example, or they might simply have not realised the signals at danger were meant for them. We shall never know.

Although the reasons for *City of Glasgow* passing danger signals were never established, the fact was that there were no devices on the train to prevent it doing so. The Great Western Railway had been installing a system called Automatic Train Protection (ATP), which alerted crews to the presence of a signal at caution or danger and then applied the brakes if they failed to acknowledge it, since 1906, but most other railways in Britain felt this was too expensive to install. A system like the Great Western's wasn't foolproof, but it might have alerted the crew of *City of Glasgow* and averted disaster.

Ironically, British Railways' own design for a system that used magnets instead of contact like the GWR's ATP was nearing the end of development – but, for the victims of Harrow, it was too late. Yet out of disaster came improvements. Harrow marked a watershed in railway safety. Since then, there has been a focus on developing and improving safety systems, meaning that to go past a red signal by more than a couple of hundred yards is now virtually impossible on the main line. It doesn't diminish the need for skilled drivers, but the latest safety systems reduce the element of human error that may well have proved so fatal at Harrow.

An eyewitness account from Geoffrey Kitchenside was uncovered by Patrick Whitehouse and David St John Thomas in *LMS 150*, and it makes uncomfortable reading:

I was in the middle of breakfast when I heard what seemed to be two distant muffled explosions a few seconds apart, and even when about ten minutes later one or two ambulances passed with bells ringing, nothing seemed exceptional. But then more ambulances, and rumours – and just 40 minutes after the event, the BBC confirmed that three trains had collided at Harrow & Wealdstone. One was a local train and the first thought was whether my father was on it, quickly denied by a telephone call.

I first saw the wreckage from the road outside the station on the Wealdstone side. It was enormous. Ambulances were lined up in the forecourt, leaving under police direction as casualties were brought out. Surprisingly the main road and shopping centre just by were not closed off. Shoppers were subdued but carried on; car drivers were seemingly oblivious of the drama.

From the road bridge at the south end of the station the enormity of the wreckage was only too apparent. The footbridge span across the fast lines linking the platforms and booking halls had disappeared. In its place was a tangled heap of wreckage with sixteen coaches compressed into the length of two spreading over the platforms onto the slow lines on the east side and across the island platform shared with the Up electric lines on the west.

What was left of two locomotives from the Liverpool train lay on their sides across the left-hand platform onto the electric lines and onto the electric line sidings. *Princess Anne* lay wrecked on her side. Somewhere underneath the mound of debris was *City of Glasgow*.

Many of the dead were railway staff who worked at Euston, but some people had miraculous escapes. The manager of Wymans bookstall was bending over a few feet from his stand to retrieve a newspaper that had blown off, when the wreckage from the second collision passed him and finished against the door of his bookstall.

The damage to the locomotives was inevitably massive, and it meant that *Windward Isles* and *Princess Anne* had to be scrapped, but *City of Glasgow* was repaired and returned to traffic, just in time for what turned out to be steam's Indian summer.

Chapter Eleven
Back on Track

The railway, like so much of Britain's infrastructure, had been hit hard by the war. Staff shortages and the need to keep critical traffic moving at all costs meant that maintenance of trains and tracks was often deferred, with just the bare minimum being done. We've already seen how speed restrictions on the West Coast Main Line during the Locomotive Exchanges prevented any useful testing being done on that route, and almost everywhere in Britain was affected similarly. Speeds had to be restricted in order for the railway to operate safely.

The amount of work needed was too great for it to be put right quickly, and back then, there were few of the 'blockades' we see today, where whole sections of line are closed for weeks, with passengers shunted onto replacement buses. Putting the tracks back in order took time, but as the 1950s progressed, rail managers were finally able to start offering the sort of service they had always wanted to.

The 1950s soon came to be regarded as a kind of Indian summer for steam. Diesel trains were being introduced here and there, but steam's hegemony wasn't seriously challenged by the new arrivals, and all of the great designs of the 'Big Four' still held sway in their respective territories. By and large, the express locomotives were cleaned well (though standards were slipping as recruitment became more difficult) and although the colours of the locomotives were different – many 'Duchesses' were painted in Brunswick Green – the spectacle remained as compelling as ever.

The period has given us many accounts, and one of the best comes from Peter Johnson, who fired and later drove 'Duchesses' from Crewe. His trilogy of books, *Through the Links at Crewe*, is a railway classic. Johnson started his railway career at Wellington, Shropshire, as a locomotive cleaner, but after transferring to the GWR shed at Crewe Gresty Lane soon fell under the spell of the LMS locomotives. After nationalisation he transferred again, this time to Crewe North, the home of a goodly fleet of 'Duchesses'. It took him a while to learn the ropes but eventually he was rostered on some of the hardest duties Crewe North had – the overnight northbound 'doodlebug' freight in particular – and it wasn't long before he had to fire his first 'Duchess', No. 46256 *Sir William A. Stanier, F.R.S.* His first experience left him shocked.

As we made our way to the roundhouse, I began to get a few butterflies in my stomach. I wondered about the spotted dick and haricot beans I had earlier but the truth was that I was realising that I had not been on the footplate of a 'Lizzie' [Crewe North's generic name for all Stanier 'Pacifics'] before let alone fired one . . . I had transferred to North Shed for greater experience and now I was certainly going to get it.

On arriving at the roundhouse I looked up at 46256, the largest locomotive I had yet to fire, and following driver Ben Woolwich, I climbed aboard; my first surprise being the size of the cab where there seemed almost enough room to ride one's bike. When I peered into the firebox my only reaction was: 'Blimey, have I got to fire this?' It looked more the size of a small ballroom.

After preparing the engine, they took it from the shed to the roundhouse and buffered up to their express from Perth. From the start, Johnson – nicknamed 'Piccolo Pete' because of his slender frame – was fighting a losing battle: 'I started shovelling and on this, my first trip with a "Lizzie", it seemed rather like giving strawberries to a donkey. I had no sooner swung a shovelful of coal into the box than whoosh! It had gone.'

Johnson now realised he was going to have to work seriously hard, but nothing he could do seemed to dent No. 46256's voracious appetite. Boiler pressure was falling as the train neared Penrith, and so was the water level as neither driver nor fireman wanted to use the injectors, which would sap more precious steam.

After a scheduled pause at Penrith, the fire was once again looking good, but whatever he did, Johnson just couldn't raise steam. They passed Shap with just 150psi on the pressure gauge, a far cry from the 250psi it was supposed to be. By Preston, where a further three coaches were added to take the load behind No. 46256 to fifteen, Johnson was thoroughly bemused: 'I had heard more than once what marvellous engines the big Stanier "Pacifics" were and yet here I was in trouble with one. There was something adrift somewhere, either with 46256 or with my firing technique, but I hadn't a clue what it was.'

At Crewe, Johnson and Woolwich were relieved by a Camden crew for the final leg to London, and Woolwich told the new men that he didn't think Johnson had been getting enough coal in the corners. 'I'll put the bladdy thing right,' said the Camden fireman.

To compound Johnson's despondency, a footplate inspector – an expert driver and fireman in his own right, and an arbiter of poor performance – was standing on the platform. The inspector recognised Johnson as the fireman who'd transferred from Crewe Gresty Lane, and softened a bit, but still wanted to get someone to show the young fireman how to master a 'Duchess'.

By this stage in his career, Johnson would have been a highly competent fireman, and indeed, except for the big 'Pacifics', had fired all the other principal ex-LMS express locomotives, so what had gone wrong? When it comes to firing a steam locomotive, it's widely held that a fireman should attempt to put coal onto the fire at the same rate the locomotive is burning it. This is called 'control firing' and it transcends the boundary between skill and art. The skill is in getting the coal to exactly where on the firebed it is needed at exactly the right time. The art is knowing where and when to do it. It's a technique also known as 'little and often' and it is a very efficient way of firing, and produces very little smoke – just a brief black puff of coal dust when the coal lands, and light grey, almost translucent smoke from the chimney. Got right, it is a thing of joy and beauty to the enginemen, as well as the accountants, to those with clean washing along the lineside, and to passengers in the train, but it doesn't leave much margin for error or mishap. Something as simple as the locomotive slipping can tear great holes in the firebed, drawing cold air through the boiler and cooling it down, cutting the steam rate. To recover means the fireman has to up his shovelling rate to compensate, and keep track of what's going on in the rest of the fire – and that adds another plate to the triumvirate of the existing fire, boiler pressure and boiler water level. In some cases, things can overwhelm even the best fireman.

And it seems this is what happened to Johnson. He fired 46256 by the book, but the firegrate on a 'Duchess' is vast, and to try to control fire it requires Herculean shovelling rates. Some of the hardest parts of the firegrate to reach are the back corners, which are the extreme left- and right-hand corners of the firebox nearest the cab. To get the coal to them, you have to put the shovelful of coal through the firehole door, and simultaneously rotate it ninety degrees and flick it as hard and fast as you can towards the corner. On the 'Duchesses' these corners are so far away from the firehole that reaching them like this is very difficult, and Johnson probably never really got enough coal into those crucial areas, which is why he was short of steam.

On the 'Duchesses' the only way most fireman could manage them was to abandon control firing on parts of the grate at least by filling them full of coal at the start of the trip and regularly topping it up. Although in theory this meant that the fire might not be burning as hot as it could be, in practice there was little noticeable difference, and it was far better to have a big blazing fire on a 'Duchess' that was really hot rather than to risk control firing and run out of steam.

After being shown the technique of getting the coal into the back corners, Johnson really mastered the 'Duchesses' and came to appreciate them for their tremendous strength and power, which proved vital on what he regarded as about the toughest passenger turn in the country, the Crewe-Perth link. He was paired with Frank Baddeley, a driver legendary for opening the throttle wide and making his fireman sweat. Even on the climb north over Shap, where these heavy trains were required to have a banking engine pushing from the rear, the 'Duchesses', when pushed, were more than able to do the job themselves:

Frank told me he would take over the shovel once we were on the move and that I could take his place. A quick hoot from the tank in the rear and an answering blast from us, then after a slight initial slip or two we began the climb – at 40% cut off and three-quarters regulator. Frank took the shovel and started piling it in then straightened up from his labours to tell me to give *Duchess of Abercorn* full regulator, and after a mile or so he took over from me.

We thundered over the summit in a crescendo of sound, smoke and steam with 46234 going great guns and still on the 235psi mark. There was three-quarters of a glass of water in the boiler and I suspect that the banker had not much to do and at times may have been hard-pressed to even keep up with us!

Baddeley worked *Duchess of Abercorn* to the limit, and although on some runs with a more light-handed driver, the fireman could sit down and have a breather from time to time, Johnson was kept hard at it. On arrival at Perth, Johnson knew he'd earned his night's rest.

But even the 'Duchesses' couldn't cope with poor coal, and on one run in particular, things didn't go Johnson and Baddeley's way. The coal clinkered rapidly, choking the fire. Clinker is what's formed when the coal has a lot of impurities – often iron pyrites – in. Above a certain temperature, these impurities melt and fuse together with the coal and ash, sealing the air gaps in the fire that feed the flames, and forming a substance that has the consistency of hard toffee when hot, and that solidifies all too rapidly when even slightly cooler. They constantly struggled for steam, and even though Baddeley tried to nurse the engine, on this southbound run they lost twenty minutes by Carstairs.

They had assistance from a tank engine over Shap summit, but the fire got worse and worse. All the crew could do was pile the coal in and draw whatever heat they could from it. On the approach to Crewe, the fire was piled as high as the brick arch in the firebox, above which are the boiler tubes the hot gases pass through – there was literally no room for any more coal to go in. On arrival at Crewe, there was so little steam pressure in the boiler that the locomotive, No. 46248 *City of Leeds*, had to be dragged on shed by a shunting engine, and the locomotive stood for days outside the shed while the fused mass of clinker was chipped out of the firebox with chisels and coal picks.

Les Jackson was also a fireman on the Crewe to Perth link, and he wrote an account of a typical run:

It was late winter 1963 and we were standing in Platform 2

at Crewe ready to work the 'Royal Highlander' [a London to Inverness express] as far as Perth, some 300 miles away non-stop. My driver was Len Basford, a good mate with over 48 years' service, nerves of steel, and a 'speed merchant' who had an uncanny way of knowing the engine's mood. Our engine was 46248 *City of Leeds*, one of Crewe North's best 'Duchesses'.

The cleaners filled the firebox with about two tons of coal (well worth a bribe of a packet of cigarettes to get them to do that!) and our train had 17 coaches weighing 610 tons, including 12-wheel sleeping cars. At departure time, 2225, I opened the dampers to get more air into the fire. The boiler pressure was 240psi, and the water was almost at the top of the boiler – if it was absolutely full, with this load the engine could prime, potentially causing major damage. Priming is where the boiler water, boiling furiously, gets carried through the regulator valve instead of steam. It then goes through the steam pipes and into the cylinders, and as water isn't compressible, can blow out the front of the cylinders if too much water is carried over.

The station staff gave us the green light for departure as the train was so long we couldn't see the guard. I closed the firebox doors to about two inches to cut the glare, and put the exhaust injector on to keep the boiler topped up and prepared for the off.

Len opened the regulator and after a short pause, as if to get the bit between her teeth, *City of Leeds* got the heavy train on the move, next stop Perth. At north junction, loco-motives can slip, but Len was already checking it before it happened. The dance of the four cylinders was getting stronger, and before long we were doing 25mph. With the train under control and accelerating, Len shortened the cut-off [equivalent to changing up a gear in a car] to 35% and put the regulator into the roof. It was time for work!

I opened the firehole door and looked at the fire through half-closed eyes to avoid being dazzled by the white-hot glow. The heat was tremendous but there was no warmth for Len as he was hanging out of the cab all the way to Perth in order to see ahead. I started a steady firing rate to keep the firebox full and the boiler pressure high. On this run, the firing was non-stop too, and if you sat down for fifteen minutes over the six hours you were lucky. Food and drink were grabbed in between shovelfuls.

We were now well on our way, having just passed Lancaster and picked up water on Hest Bank troughs. On this level stretch, we sped in the high 80s towards Carnforth, where the real climbing begins. To make matters worse, we were heading into the teeth of a snow storm and gale force winds. I wasn't worried as we had a masterpiece of engineering in the 'Duchess' and an expert driver. I increased the firing rate to keep pace with demand for steam from the boiler, and Len dropped the cut-off further to 30%, regulator still wide open as we passed Oxenholme.

It's at times like this when you seem to have a feeling for the engine – steam in the blood you might call it – and you start talking to her. 'Come on old girl,' I said. I know it's only metal, but over the years, I have found that if you treat locomotives like ladies – electrics included – it pays dividends.

We were speeding towards Tebay, and collected water

from Dillacar troughs. In a storm like this, you have to know all the little landmarks – through the rock cutting, over the river bridge, lift the water scoop. Len asked if I needed a banking engine, but I was fine, and in any case, a driver worth his salt on a trip like this thought it was a slight against his skill to have one.

We started climbing Shap hoping there was nothing stuck ahead of us that would cause us to stop – things don't always go to plan! – and Len lengthened the cut-off to 40%, like changing from fifth gear to fourth in a car when going uphill. Anyone standing by the lineside couldn't fail to be filled with emotion to see such a machine pounding away, the smoke from the exhaust rising 50 feet into the night sky, the glare from the firebox stabbing the night sky like a giant search-light, and I was shovelling the coal in like a conveyor belt, such was the demand for steam.

The water in the boiler had fallen to about half-full so I increased the rate of the injectors to keep up. 'Come on, old girl, two miles to go and then you can have a breather,' I said. Then we were into the rock cutting 500 yards short of the summit, hoping and praying that it wasn't blocked with snow. Len put the sanders on to increase grip and put his hand on the regulator in anticipation. Sure enough, within 30 seconds 46248 slipped, but Len was ready for it and stopped the slip almost before it started. I asked how he knew, and he said he had a premonition it would slip (something I would find out for myself on 46229 *Duchess of Hamilton* in the same place many years later).

By now the cut-off was 55% as we laboured over Shap, passing the signalbox at 27mph. Despite our gallant efforts the summit and snow storm had beat us. We were running three minutes late at the top, and had to get that back, so we stormed down the bank towards Penrith and Carlisle, touching 86mph in places [there was no 80mph speed restriction for passenger comfort on sleeper coaches in those days!]. We passed Carlisle and headed north over the 1-in-65 to Beattock, hoping the snowploughs had been out, Len preparing for a slip which thankfully didn't come.

By now we were on the home straight, and as we passed first Stirling and then Bridge of Allan I was getting tired, shovelling in a trance, every joint aching, legs like jelly and as black as a panda. I was longing for a warm bed, but there was still work to do. The fire was getting clinkered – something unavoidable on a long run like this – so we broke it up using the dart and managed to keep the steam pressure at 225psi for the last few miles into Perth, where we were relieved by another crew.

It's a funny feeling when you step down onto the platform after a non-stop run like that after feeling the power of the locomotive, rocking and rolling under your feet. Whenever we walked away from the locomotive I always looked back with a lump in my throat, at what I think is the best thing ever invented by man.

Les Jackson is typical of so many engine crew who regarded their locomotives as willing beasts, almost friends, rather than the often temperamental lumps of machinery they could be. At the time, he would never have believed that, more than thirty years later, he would play a dramatic and fondly regarded part in the 'Duchess' story.

But if trips like Les Jackson's were the bread-and-butter work of 'Duchesses', it was equally possible to see these giants hauling local trains of only a few carriages between Crewe, Shrewsbury, Wellington and Stafford, a duty about as far removed from the Perth jobs as can be imagined. The reason was simple: back before Beeching wielded his axe, those lines formed part of a circular route from Crewe, and it was a perfect way of ensuring overhauls at the works had been carried out properly.

Just like a new car, when a steam locomotive is over-hauled, all the tolerances in the joints, pistons, cylinders and valves are at their minimum, and can be very tight. It would have been crazy to send a locomotive straight out of Crewe Works onto something like the Perth trips, so all loco-motives had to be comprehensively run in before they were allowed onto top-link duties.

Stanier, meanwhile, continued to take an active interest in railways, and Brian Radford, who is now Chief Engineer of the Princess Royal Class Locomotive Trust, but was then an apprentice at Derby Works, recalls meeting him:

'It was a real honour to meet Sir William, and he wasn't aloof at all. He was into his 70s by then, but he was still very sharp and took particular interest in the apprentices, asking questions about what we were doing, and wishing us well – he was a genuinely good guy.'

Simply running a locomotive by itself wouldn't test all the systems, particularly the braking and train heating, and rather than haul an empty train around for the sake of it, it was just common sense to use Crewe's output on local trains that weren't travelling too far away from the works. In that part of the world, a trip down to Shrewsbury, then across to Stafford via Wellington and up the West Coast Main Line to Crewe was a good way of testing the full range of the locomotive's capabilities. My father, Gordon Roden, was a lad in short trousers in the 1950s, but seeing the 'Duchesses', 'Princess Royals', 'Royal Scots' and others pass through his local station at Donnington made a profound impression on him and others. Rather than getting normal bedtime stories as a child, I listened to my father tell me about these giant locomotives that he'd seen as a kid, and of their tremendous feats on the main line – as a child of the 1980s, this was the stuff of legend, and far more thrilling than hearing about some bulked-up hero slaying dragons.

These are his memories, and they'll be similar to those of many others:

My first memory of any steam engine was on my annual holiday to Scotland with my parents in about 1955. Having walked about a mile-and-a-half to my local station at Donnington, I must have been pretty tired because I can remember nothing else until Crewe at about 2300 and watching these large maroon or green engines glide into the platform. I was hooked.

There, with my father and elder brother, we watched in awe, and though I can't have been more than three or so, I wasn't the least bit scared, except on the occasion when the train expected ('The Royal Highlander') grumbled in with a light blue diesel called *Deltic* that made what I thought at the time was a horrible noise. I had to hide behind my father's legs until this monstrosity had gone and normal proper engines were the order of the day again.

'Duchesses' held sway on the West Coast, and I was privileged to travel behind these gentle giants of steam all the way to Carlisle or Glasgow where they gave way to smaller engines for the remainder of the journey to Elgin.

Later on in my life, trainspotting was a hobby most boys had back then and it wasn't long before my brother and I were venturing to Shrewsbury or Stafford on sorties to spot some 'namers'. I suppose we were very lucky in that at Shrewsbury we could get up-close to 'Duchesses' running ex-works from Crewe: you could even smell the fresh paint along with all the other aromas of a steam engine.

This is the sort of stuff I was brought up on – no wonder I felt I'd been born thirty years too late!

In the 1950s in particular, trainspotting was a near-universal hobby for children all over Britain, and with the likes of the 'Duchesses' pounding the rails, it's easy to see why. As a spectacle, even though it was an everyday scene, it encompassed all the things children and small boys in particular love – noise, speed, power, the sensation of a heavy train passing, and of course, dirt. No wonder they flocked to linesides and stations in their droves to see it, and on the West Coast Main Line, which by the mid-1950s was finally starting to be rid of many of the speed restrictions that had plagued it since the war, things were about to get even better for the lineside observers: British Railways was getting serious about speed.

Chapter Twelve
Speed and Sojourns

The wear and tear inflicted on Britain's railways during the war caused a huge maintenance backlog to build up, and with continuing heavy traffic, it took a long time for the tracks to be safe enough for the operating authorities to risk faster schedules, but when they did, the old competition between the West and East Coast routes kicked off in earnest after a seventeen-year ceasefire.

The Eastern Region broke the armistice first in 1956 with a new train called 'The Talisman', which was booked for 6½ hours between London and Edinburgh Waverley. It was a significant acceleration of services, and the London Midland Region was compelled to respond, both by commercial imperatives to maintain loadings on the lucrative London-Scotland trains, and by the need to be seen to be as good as, if not better than, its rivals across the country.

The West Coast Main Line's answer to 'The Talisman' came the following year, 1957, with the launch of 'The Caledonian' from London to Glasgow. It was ambitious stuff given the circumstances. There was just one intermediate stop at Carlisle, and the 6 hrs 40 min schedule for the 401 miles was only ten minutes longer than the streamlined 'Coronation Scot', which ceased running at the outbreak of war in 1939 and never resumed. Unlike the 'Coronation Scot' it was timed to appeal to businessmen, leaving Euston at 0830 and returning from Glasgow at 1615.

On 15 June 1957, *Duchess of Hamilton* pulled out of London Euston with the first 'Caledonian', the swirl of bagpipes echoing around the ancient and increasingly dilapidated station. The train's average speed of 61.7mph was faster than that of 'The Talisman' and the non-stop distance from London to Carlisle of 299 miles was longer than its rival's equivalent, which saw locomotives changed at Newcastle.

From the start the train proved popular, and in an echo of the 'races to the north' of the late nineteenth and early twentieth centuries, the London Midland Region was determined to extract the maximum publicity value from its fastest train. On 5 September 1957, trains running ahead of 'The Caledonian' were discreetly sidelined in order to guarantee a clear run from Glasgow to Euston aimed at setting a new record between the two cities. The locomotive chosen was No. 46244 *King George VI* and by Crewe, the train was already thirteen minutes ahead of schedule.

Sadly no detailed record of the run has survived, but we can get some idea of just how good parts of it were from the guard's log, which timed it to the nearest half-minute. The final sixty miles from Roade to Euston took around forty-three minutes, and from Bletchley to Tring, it's been estimated that the average speed was 93mph. *King George VI* arrived at Euston in just 6 hrs 3 mins, a whopping thirty-seven minutes ahead of schedule, and the final 158 miles from Crewe saw a gain of twenty-four minutes made against schedule – the same time as that of *Coronation* in 1937, and of the first standard electric schedules introduced in 1966.

With such a huge margin over the published schedule, you might think that the opportunity would have been taken to cut journey times further, but it wasn't, and it took until the 1970s to improve on this. If the powers that were seemed overly cautious, there was some sort of method in their madness, because, as we've seen, the West Coast Main Line didn't really have enough 'Duchesses' to guarantee one at all times. The trains had to be within the capability of one of the second-line 'Royal Scot' or 'Jubilee' 4-6-0s to take over if need be. It was a different story on the East Coast Main Line, where 'Pacifics' were the norm (it would have been a rare event indeed for anything less than a 'V2' to haul a long-distance express to Scotland on that line).

'The Caledonian' was a brief last chance for the big Stanier 'Pacifics' to show what they could do, but even by 1958, the game was up as preparations gathered for the greatest change on Britain's railways since Stephenson's *Rocket*. The schedule was expanded to 6 hrs 55 min because it had been decided to electrify the southern portion of the West Coast Main Line from London to Crewe, and that meant an awful lot of disruptive engineering work.

The 1950s also saw some of the 'Duchesses' make occasional sojourns to their designer's home territory, the Western Region. By then the 'Kings' were getting on in years, and the stresses imposed by their huge bulk were beginning to tell. As more and more were withdrawn for repair, the Western Region found itself short of its most powerful locomotives. In a bid to see whether there were any alternatives, No. 46237 *City of Bristol* was transferred to the area on 19 April 1955, but despite the clear Swindon ancestry of the locomotive, she wasn't well received. According to *The Railway Observer*, the magazine of the Railway Correspondence and Travel Society, a London Midland Region locomotive inspector was rather nonplussed about the 'Duchess' being used on the nine-coach 'Merchant Venturer' from London Paddington to Bristol: after all, she'd hauled seventeen coaches from Carlisle to Euston the week before, and it must have seemed like a waste of the locomotive's power.

While arrival in Bristol was a little late, rather more embarrassing problems presented themselves at Bristol Bath Road, the Western Region's primary shed in the area. The locomotive had to be turned, but on the shed's first turntable, she was too long, straddling the turntable and preventing it moving round. In the exasperated spirit of railwaymen around the world, they tried her on the other turntable, with the same result. There was only one way to turn the locomotive – she had to travel out to the triangle at North Somerset Junction, reverse around the top side, and, now facing in the opposite direction, reverse back so she was facing London. After that charade, she was used on trains to Plymouth and Birkenhead, where she could be turned more easily.

The following year, the 'Kings' were again in trouble, this time with fatigue cracking in their bogies. This time the Western Region acted decisively, taking the whole fleet out of service progressively from late January to the end of February to effect repairs. To replace them the London Midland Region sent three 'Pacifics' – No. 46210 *Princess Patricia*, No. 46254 *City of Stoke-on-Trent* and No. 46257 *City of Salford*. They worked the same sorts of duties as No. 46237 a year before, and while their performances were unspectacular, they showed they could easily match the Western Region's own fleet.

Even by the time the brief holiday on the Western Region had started, let alone 'The Caledonian', it was becoming ever more clear that steam was approaching its twilight years. In a bid to redress growing losses on the railways, it was decided to unleash the latest products of Britain's industry on the railways. In a way, it foresaw Harold Wilson's famous quote of a few years later: 'The Britain that is going to be forged in the white heat of this revolution will be no place for restrictive practices or for outdated methods on either side of industry.' Given that the railway was one of the most conservative industries ever, it was to come as quite a shock to the system.

Chapter Thirteen
Modernisation!

Throughout the 1950s, the financial state of British Railways was a perennial concern for the government, as costs soared and traffic was lost to road competition. At a time when iconic futuristic aircraft like the Vulcan bomber and Hawker Hunter were taking to the skies, the steam railway looked very old-fashioned and inefficient. Time, then, for a plan.

Forced to find ways of cutting mounting losses, British Railways decided on an all-or-nothing gamble to modernise its network as quickly as possible. The result of its thinking was released in 1955 as the Modernisation Plan and it was nothing short of breathtaking in its scope and ambition. The thinking was straightforward: as steam locomotives were expensive to operate, service and maintain (although they were cheap to build) they would be replaced by diesel and electric alternatives. In the south, the existing third-rail electrified network would be extended to eliminate steam, while the West and East Coast Main Lines would be wired for electric traction. (In the event, the whole West Coast Main Line wasn't completed until the 1970s, and the East Coast not until 1991). Everywhere else would receive diesel trains to hold the fort until the wires or third-rails reached them.

It was reasoned that, despite their greater cost, diesel and electric trains were cheaper to run overall than steam as they could operate around the clock (no need to empty smoke-boxes there) and would require less servicing. They would also in many cases be faster and more powerful, allowing reductions in journey times to attract passengers and freight customers.

Replacing steam with diesel and electric trains was hardly a leap of the imagination: the Southern Railway had been gradually doing it with electrification for many years, and diesel shunting locomotives were entering service in goods yards around the country, bringing great savings in the process. On many local services too, motorised diesel carriages called multiple units were replacing one-, two- and three-coach local trains to great effect. The big question was how to replace the top-line freight, passenger and general-purpose steam locomotives with the new technologies.

Half the problem was deciding exactly what the require-ments were for diesel locomotives in the first place. This was why the LMS had ordered 10000 and 10001 just before nationalisation – to see how the best the British diesel manufacturing industry could build compared with the 'Duchesses', and a number of other prototype diesels had been ordered with that in mind. BR's own CME, Robert Riddles, probably had the right idea in the early 1950s, by using a new generation of steam locomotives to replace the many anachronisms still running on the railway first of all, then, as diesel technology was perfected, in turn replacing these steam locomotives as they became life-expired. The need to modernise was not in question.

The logic was right, but although British Railways was a single entity in name, in practice its division into regions largely approximating to those of the pre-nationalisation companies (with the exception of Scotland, which had its own region now) meant that pre-1948 cultures still held sway — and that meant, inevitably, that the 'Big Four' areas would all go their separate ways when it came to deciding precisely how to modernise.

So, the Southern Region continued its policy of electrification and by and large ignored diesels, while the Western Region opted for light, powerful, high-revving diesel-hydraulics to replace its steam fleet, which in many cases would have been due for replacement anyway. It was on the two principal north-south main lines that fundamental differences of philosophy came to the fore. As they say, old habits die hard.

The first products of the Modernisation Plan that could really supplant the big steam locomotives were the English Electric Type 4 diesels. These were big, bulky locomotives but they had 2,000hp engines, so on a nominal basis they were roughly the equal of the 'Duchesses' on the West Coast and the 'A1', 'A3' and 'A4' 'Pacifics' on the East Coast, and it was the latter that got them first. The Eastern Region found them to be moderately reliable, and certainly possessed of greater availability than its steam fleet, but the real measure of a diesel locomotive's power is what it can put down on the rails, and the losses incurred by the Type 4's generator, which the engine turned to drive electric traction motors on the wheels, brought the 2,000hp of the engine down to 1,550hp. This meant that one of the star attractions of the new technologies — the potential for accelerating journey times — couldn't be brought to bear as the existing steam fleet was well able to match this.

The Eastern Region wasn't satisfied with equilibrium with the steam fleet, and ordered a small batch of 3,300hp diesels based on a prototype called *Deltic*, which operated successfully across Britain in the 1950s. The 'Deltics' were expensive and temperamental machines, but their huge power and 100mph speed meant that the investment could generate worthwhile speed increases.

The London Midland Region's problem was rather more pronounced. Although the Type 4s were the most powerful 1950s diesel passenger locomotives, the 'Duchesses' were even more powerful in the hands of a good crew, and with electrification scheduled for completion by the mid-1960s, it was impossible to justify ordering a fleet of 'Deltics' for its own purposes. In the end, the LMR ordered Type 4s, as there was nothing else available – there would be no major journey time improvements on the cards here.

Further down the power scale, things followed the same pattern. Smaller diesel locomotives in the Type 2 category were roughly equivalent to a 'Black 5' mixed-traffic engine in terms of power at around 949hp at rail, but rather than order some of the forthcoming English Electric Type 3s, whose extra 301hp of power would have made a meaningful improvement, opted to order dozens of Type 2s, arguing that as one crew could control multiple locomotives coupled together, it could always double-head if need be. It was the Midland Railway's small-engine policy writ large on a big-engine railway that has always demanded more powerful locomotives than anywhere else.

That the 'Duchesses' were able to match the diesels is

illustrated in a comparison made in the January 1959 issue of *Trains Illustrated*. The steam locomotive was No. 46221 *Queen Elizabeth*, and the diesel was the prototype English Electric locomotive 10203, whose 1,550hp power at rail was the same as the Type 4s later introduced. Loadings behind the two locomotives were almost identical, so between Glasgow and Crewe, this was as fair a comparison as can be made.

The diesel covered the 12.9 miles to Motherwell in 18 min 4 secs; *Queen Elizabeth* in 17 mins 50 secs; by Law Junction, the diesel was sixteen seconds ahead, but by Carstairs, forty-one miles from Glasgow, this lead had been cut to eight seconds, despite a temporary speed restriction of 15mph hindering *Queen Elizabeth*. Beattock summit was passed just over a minute faster by the diesel than by steam, but this was due to another speed restriction affecting *Queen Elizabeth*. Other logs paint the same picture – the difference between diesel and steam on the West Coast Main Line was down to signal checks and speed restrictions rather than the locomotives.

If performance was identical, surely it made more sense to keep the steam locomotives and their crews on the duties they knew so well and use the diesels to accelerate less demanding services – especially given that the diesels themselves would be displaced once electrification was complete. Despite this, the tendency was for the diesels to replace top-link steam locomotives like the 'Duchesses' first.

And this really is where the absurdities of the Modernisation Plan came to the fore. Yes, replace steam with diesel by all means, especially on lighter duties where diesels could replace huge numbers of lesser-powered steam locomotives – but when in timing terms steam was to be replaced by electric traction, why go to all the effort of retraining staff twice, and of building new facilities that might not really be needed in a few years? It remains one of the great controversies of the Modernisation Plan – that serviceable, modern, efficient steam locomotives were replaced like-for-like on top-link express passenger duties when there were potentially real gains to be made in replacing lower-powered locomotives and accelerating the services they hauled.

Oddly, BR did little to address some of its other costs: even small stations had full complements of staff, and there are places without railways today that might have retained them had the stations been de-staffed and operations simplified.

All of this happened before the infamous Dr Beeching got stuck into the railways, and for the London Midland Region's front-line express steam locomotives – the 'Duchesses' and 'Princess Royals' – it meant early withdrawal as the dogma of dieselisation became ever more entrenched.

Chapter Fourteen
Giants Slain

Although the early diesels took their time in entering service, at the start of the 1960s, the days of top-link (the most demanding duties, given to the best crews) express passenger steam were numbered across the whole of Britain. The Eastern Region had already started culling its older and less able 'Pacifics' by the turn of the decade, and the Western Region was looking ominously at the 'Kings'.

All the top-link express locomotives bar some on the Southern Region, which wanted to complete its electrification programme and jump from steam to electric with few diesels, were now in the firing line, and it didn't take long for the first Stanier 'Pacifics' to be put against the wall. Four of the ten 'Princess Royals' were withdrawn in October 1961 as the diesels made them apparently redundant. The remainder hung on for another year, but by November 1962 all had been withdrawn, and most would be scrapped within weeks.

As the run-down gathered pace, the 'Duchesses' increasingly found themselves marginalised, either operating on the likes of the sleeper trains to Perth, or on parcels or even goods traffic. Some, though, found use as standby locomotives at places like Liverpool, ready to take over from failed diesels. The diesels were suffering from a combination of the usual unreliability of new technology, the dirt of the steam railway and the unfamiliarity of crews with their new charges, but if a 'Duchess' was in steam at crucial locations, there was every chance trains could keep to time.

Many crews welcomed the diesels as the working environment was so much better. The driver could sit down, had a good view of the track ahead and didn't have to contend with the draughts, vibration, physical labour and dirt of a steam footplate. Given a choice, many drivers opted for the new locomotives more than willingly. For the firemen, there was nothing much to do, but they were retained as 'secondmen' in the cab as it was felt that with so little to do physically, there was a danger that drivers might fall asleep or miss crucial signals.

From 1962, any locomotives that needed major repairs on boilers, frames and so on were withdrawn, and three 'Duchesses' (No. 46227 *Duchess of Devonshire*, No. 46231 *Duchess of Atholl* and No. 46232 *Duchess of Montrose*) were withdrawn at the same time as their cousin 'Princess Royals', in autumn 1962. And then there was a brief stay of execution for the 'Duchesses'. Across the country, the same thing was happening. The Great Western 'Kings' had all been withdrawn by the end of 1962, and the Eastern was eliminating 'A3s' rapidly and had started making inroads into the 'A4s' with five withdrawn by the end of 1962. Seven years after the Modernisation Plan was announced, express steam was in headlong retreat.

Inevitably the appearance of the locomotives suffered, as the effects of the Modernisation Plan, combined with near-crippling shortages of labour, made their mark. Although it was possible to see fairly clean 'Duchesses' to the end, increasingly they – and many other locomotives across the country – looked tired and ready for the scrapman. Even so, when a Type 4 diesel failed just before hauling the Royal Train from Euston to an overnight stabling point in Lancashire, No. 46248 *City of Leeds* was taken out of store at Crewe North, fettled up and rostered to this prestigious duty. On the following day, 14 December, No. 46220 *Coronation* hauled the train to Liverpool Lime Street – an appropriate engine indeed. Oddly, the 'Duchesses' weren't often used on the Royal Train because, just like today, the railway prefers to have two locomotives hauling the train in case one fails: it wouldn't do to delay a member of the Royal Family because of a failure, so often a pair of lower-powered locomotives like the 'Black 5s' were used instead.

Nineteen sixty-three is famous – perhaps notorious is a better word – for what's since been known universally as the 'Beeching Cuts'. The head of the British Transport Commission, Dr (later Lord) Richard Beeching was tasked with returning the railways to financial health because the Modernisation Plan wasn't delivering the savings it was claimed it would. Beeching proposed radical action, culling unprofitable lines – often using a flawed methodology – around the country, and axing services that would today be considered highly useful. His actions were targeted further down the food chain than the West Coast Main Line, however, so for once this is a story of the steam railway where the good doctor is an innocent bystander.

Despite the diesels – and because of their continued unreliability, 'Duchesses' still worked named trains like 'The Caledonian' and 'The Royal Scot' on occasion, and the Carlisle locomotives often worked from Glasgow St Enoch to Carlisle. Other duties that still fell to the fleet included the London to Holyhead 'Irish Mail'. After a brief pause, withdrawals resumed in 1963, with No. 46234 *Duchess of Abercorn* – the record-breaker – retired in January of that cold winter, though she would remain intact for another six months. The pioneer of the class, No. 46220 *Coronation*, was taken out of service in April and scrapped just a month later. Others in the same boat in the first third of the year included No. 46246 *City of Manchester* and No. 46253 *City of St. Albans*. By May 1963 there were just twenty-nine of the thirty-seven in service.

And it continued. In May, No. 46221 *Queen Elizabeth* went, followed by No. 46247 *City of Liverpool* and No. 46252 *City of Leicester* in June. Summer holidays must have taken effect then, because the fleet remained intact until October, when four were taken out of service. No longer could trainspotters underline No. 46222 *Queen Mary*, No. 46223 *Princess Alice*, No. 46224 *Princess Alexandra* or No. 46242 *City of Glasgow* in their books. Two more, No. 46230 *Duchess of Buccleuch* and No. 46249 *City of Sheffield*, went in November before another ceasefire was called. It sounds bad, but by comparison with the armageddon that was happening on most of the other express fleets, to have twenty-two in traffic at the start of 1964 was quite something: there were only nineteen 'A4s' on the Eastern Region. On the Southern Region, the 'Merchant Navys' (by now thoroughly rebuilt in conventional form) remained intact, but even they would soon start to be cut back.

At the same time as electrification, British Railways took the opportunity to thoroughly modernise stations along the route. Birmingham New Street, with its damaged and worn glass overall roof, was gutted to make way for the rabbit warren of a station we have today. Coventry, Stafford, Nuneaton and many others all gained a new concrete and glass style of building that seemed to ape the feel of airline terminals. And then there was Euston, which, unlike the others, really did need modernising. The outcry over the demolition of the famous Doric Arch and accompanying Great Hall in 1962 overlooked the fact that Euston was a complex, difficult to operate and chaotic station that could achieve much more with a simpler layout. At the time there was a general attitude of moving on from the past, something seen with the redevelopment of towns and cities around the country, so it was hardly surprising the railway would want to reflect the mood. Despite protests, the old Euston buildings were demolished, and in their place emerged a station that, despite its many critics, is easy to use and navigate for passengers, and easy to operate for the railway. Its light, airy concourse is rather like that of Berlin Tempelhof airport, and if it weren't for the invasive clutter of retail units that plagues every railway station these days, would actually be a really impressive space. Euston was emblematic of the West Coast upgrade, and when it was shiny and new, it must have seemed like a leap into the future. In a way, I think it still does.

The gradual displacement of the 'Duchesses' wasn't as rapid as for their counterparts on the Eastern Region, and they could still be seen working express trains into London Euston and Glasgow, as well as stopping trains. Into 1964 they still covered most of their old hunting grounds, but the prestige of the locomotives didn't prevent their use on fish and cattle trains and even trains of empty coal wagons.

Two locomotives were withdrawn in February that year, No. 46229 *Duchess of Hamilton* and No. 46233 *Duchess of Sutherland*, which had both been bought by the holiday camp legend Billy Butlin (of which more later). The London Midland Region was still able to extract good work from the remaining twenty 'Duchesses' and it seems that it was prepared to keep them running as a number had been put through works recently for overhaul – not an expense one would go to for a locomotive at the end of its working life. But the railway didn't work so logically then and in July 1964 an edict was issued stating that all of the remaining 'Duchesses' were to be withdrawn from 12 September. On that date they would work to their home sheds and have their names and numberplates removed.

In anticipation of their imminent demise, a number of enthusiast specials ran, taking members of the class over the old Great Central line from Nottingham to Didcot, and from Shrewsbury to Paddington.

As September started, the last rites took place. On 1 September, No. 46243 *City of Lancaster* worked the 1130 Birmingham to Edinburgh, the last of the fleet to visit the Scottish capital on a scheduled service, and on 4 September, No. 46238 *City of Carlisle* hauled 'The Caledonian' – the last

'Duchess' to do so. Appearances of the type over those last few days were sporadic, with No. 46228 *Duchess of Rutland* the last of the class into Glasgow Central, but on 12 September, all bar No. 46256 *Sir William A. Stanier, F.R.S.* were nominally taken out of service, though some survived a couple of days beyond that.

No. 46256 had been retained for a special train for the RTCS on 26 September 1964 from Crewe to Carlisle, where Eastern Region 'A4' No. 60007 *Sir Nigel Gresley* took over. This now-legendary tour took in the direct Carlisle to Edinburgh 'Waverley' route (a much-missed line) and proved a suitable 'last hurrah' for the 'Duchesses'. No. 46256 wasn't scrapped immediately, however; she was stored at Crewe because a preservation bid was pending. It would have been marvellous if she'd been saved – and I'd suggest that she should have been for the National Collection – but the buyer was unable to stump up the £2,500 BR wanted, then chose another engine, and failed to buy that too.

It seems the 'Duchesses' were considered instead of the remaining 'A4s' from the Eastern Region to work trains on the steeply graded and demanding line to Dundee and Aberdeen, a line that had seen even the Eastern Region's 'Pacifics' struggle. Whether it was a decision based on personal preference, or just that crews in the area were familiar with the 'A4s', it was decided that the flagships of the West Coast Main Line would not eke out their remaining careers in Scotland. The axe was looming. The two Butlin's 'Duchesses' and No. 46235 *City of Birmingham* (which would be displayed at Birmingham Museum of Science and Industry) would be the only of their type to survive.

Another 'giant' who passed away in this period was Sir William Stanier himself. He had suffered a slight stroke in 1961, and the following year the Institute of Mechanical Engineers awarded him the prestigious James Watt International Medal. When his namesake locomotive was withdrawn, he accepted one of its nameplates, intending to mount one in his study, but it was too long for the wall! He died in September 1965, aged 89. He had outlived his finest creations in service, but had survived long enough to know that one at least was saved for posterity, and another two were safe for the time being. After a slightly shaky start to his tenure at the LMS, he had given his name to one of the world's truly great locomotive designs, and was loved and revered even by those who had never travelled behind them. Sir Frank Mason gave the address at his funeral:

> William Stanier is an outstanding example of someone who remained young at heart all his days and one of his secrets was that he always had time for the younger man. He was able, therefore, to guide and influence younger people. I know, because I am one.
>
> With this youthfulness went a flexibility of mind which enabled him to keep up-to-date professionally. His approach to everything was simple and direct as befits an engineer, and he combined this with understanding and kindliness and courage. A wonderful recipe for greatness.

The 'Duchesses' that didn't make it into preservation

were scrapped quickly, many at Crewe Works, the place that built them, though some were scrapped at private sites such as the West of Scotland Shipbreaking Company at Troon, and at J Cashmore, Great Bridge, particularly the locomotives withdrawn in 1964. To see a steam locomotive being scrapped is like watching an animal being slaughtered. In those days, when health and safety regulations were few, the 'gas axe' – an oxyacetylene torch – was king, and the scrapping process was brutal.

After all the easy-to-remove components had been taken off, such as gauges, handrails and so on, the scrapmen tore into the carcasses of the 'Duchesses'. There was little orderly disassembly, though one presumes Crewe Works kept useable components from the earliest withdrawn 'Duchesses' for use on the survivors if needed. With the scrapmen standing wherever they could find a perch, the flames of the blowtorches cut through the precision-made and assembled parts of the 'Duchesses' easily. Invariably work started at the top, on the boiler. When holes were torched in the sides of the boiler to gain access to the boiler tubes, it was like ripping open the locomotive's heart – the arteries that once carried hot gas from the firebox through the boiler were burned through and cast aside, the fireboxes that almost defeated so many firemen were chopped into pieces, and bit by bit over a few days, perhaps longer, the process continued until all that was left of the locomotive was an anonymous pile of scrap metal.

Some of the metal was melted down and used in new diesel locomotives, but more was sold to the highest bidder.

The valuable copper of the firebox had little use in a diesel locomotive save for wires, and was worth a small fortune on the open market. It was an unpleasant way for the loco-motives to end, but the withdrawal of steam locomotives meant a bonanza for the scrapmen: they, at least, had never had it so good.

The mass cull of the 'Duchesses' robbed the railway of one of its greatest spectacles, and the 'Duchesses' were mourned from the bustling capital through the Trent Valley, and all the great cities they once called at, but nowhere were they missed more than the grand fells of Shap and Beattock. No more charging down Shap at 110mph with a sleeper train; no more gigantic power outputs; no more firemen pitting their skills against the elements to take massive passenger trains over Britain's most important railway, in speed, safety and style. When the last fire was dropped, it marked the end of one of the most spectacular periods in railway history. Thanks to Billy Butlin and Birmingham Museum of Science and Industry, people would still be able to admire the size and grace of a 'Duchess' but it would be like a silent opera – the most important elements of move-ment and sound and spectacle would all be missing, and the world was a poorer place for it.

Chapter Fifteen
Beside the Sea ...

The last 'Duchesses' were withdrawn forty-four years ago, in 1964, and, as they say, the past is a different country. Britain was very different from today. Cynics might suggest that we had a manufacturing industry back then, but the differences were far more profound. We ate differently – diets, though perhaps healthier, were far less varied and cosmopolitan than many people's are today. We dressed differently, we worked differently and we entertained ourselves differently.

Television was far from universal – many families still managed quite happily without, and those that couldn't had to make do with two channels until April. Amongst the top shows on TV were *Steptoe and Son*, *Sunday Palladium* and *Take Your Pick*, though for hip young things, *Top of the Pops*, mercifully, had started earlier that year. In February, when *Duchess of Hamilton* and *Duchess of Sutherland* were withdrawn, you'd have found Cilla Black at the top of the charts with 'Anyone Who Had a Heart'. And if you were in the United States, you couldn't have escaped Beatlemania.

The differences extended to the way we travelled. Although motor cars were soaring in popularity, it wouldn't be for another twenty or so years that ownership started to reach universality, and that meant people had to travel by public transport. Foreign travel was rare, aside from the odd trip to

France, and air travel overwhelmingly the preserve of the wealthy leisured, or very important businessmen, and that meant that when Britons went on holiday, they stayed in Britain. For thousands if not millions of people in that period, holidays could mean only one thing – a week or two at Butlin's.

The founder of Butlin's, Billy Butlin, was born in 1899 into a showbusiness family and he opened his first holiday camp in Skegness in 1936, aiming to provide a good-value, entertaining break to the masses. It was a spectacular success, and by 1964, the year he was knighted, Billy Butlin had seven holiday camps dotted around the country at seaside resorts. It's fashionable these days to poke fun at these institutions, with their knobbly knee contests and redcoats (*Hi-de-Hi!* has a lot to answer for) but the simple fact is that holidaymakers flocked to the camps and had a jolly good time while they were there.

Butlin was a consummate entrepreneur, and he couldn't fail to have seen the popularity of trainspotting over the 1950s and early 1960s. Indeed, there were miniature railways at some of his camps that proved very popular. When the rail enthusiast Brian Walker began writing to Sir Billy suggesting that some of the giants of steam could make popular exhibits at the camps, he found that the company was prepared to consider the suggestion. The 6201 Princess Elizabeth Locomotive Society had bought that locomotive in 1963, and was actively raising funds to purchase No. 6100 *Royal Scot*.

Butlin's Assistant Managing Director, G.S. Ogg, gave a positive response, suggesting that the company would be happy to display the locomotives, but in February that year, the board rejected the idea because of the need to spend

£15,000. Walker persisted, and persuaded Butlin's to rethink, this time with a view to acquiring its own loco-motives. Butlin wanted big passenger locomotives with significant history, and made a bid for 'Princess Royal' No. 46203 *Princess Margaret Rose*, which had been withdrawn the year before. The bid was successful and in May Ogg wrote to Walker confirming the purchase. He revealed that No. 46203 would be sent to Pwllheli, Wales, for display – and that they were negotiating for No. 6100 *Royal Scot*, which would be shown at Skegness.

Princess Margaret Rose was moved quickly, arriving in Wales the same month she was bought. *Royal Scot* followed soon after, arriving in Skegness in July 1963. It was to prove a remarkably well-judged decision on the part of Ogg and Butlin. Both knew their customers inside out, and the crowds that flocked to both locomotives – even though you could still see equivalents on the operating railway – vindicated their decision. What Ogg realised was that many of the younger campers in 1963 were avid trainspotters, and one of their dreams would have been to stand in the cab of a front-line express locomotive – a dream that only Butlin's could fulfil. They also probably had an idea that many rail enthusiasts from the 1940s had young kids of their own – and these locomotives could act as another draw to the parents.

Pleased with the reception granted to the first two steam locomotives, Butlin's sought to acquire more for its camps at Minehead and Ayr. Still with glamorous locomotives in mind, they approached British Railways to buy the first streamlined 'A4' No. 60014 *Silver Link*. It would have been fabulous for this locomotive to be preserved, but BR wanted a price way above the locomotive's scrap value, and Butlin's, ever with an eye on the bank balance, declined to pay over the odds. Plan 'B' was to try to buy a 'King' of the Great Western Railway, presumably for display at Minehead. They bid for No. 6018 *King Henry VI* but again BR was greedy and instead the locomotive was scrapped.

Ogg wasn't to be defeated, and this time he went to the London Midland Region, which had started withdrawing the 'Duchesses'. He wanted No. 46220 *Coronation*, but when Walker pointed out that it was actually No. 46229 *Duchess of Hamilton* that had gone to America, he opted for her instead. The London Midland Region was far more amenable and agreed a price for the locomotive, which was destined for Minehead. By now knowing that 'Duchesses' were available at a sensible cost, and that campers were unlikely to visit Minehead and Ayr, Butlin's bought No. 46233 *Duchess of Sutherland*, for display at the Ayr camp in Scotland. A few small tank engines were also bought to complete a hugely significant line-up of locomotives. The two 'Duchesses' were cosmetically restored at Crewe in a version of the LMS maroon they looked so well in (though, strictly speaking, it was incorrect for *Duchess of Hamilton* as she was streamlined for most of her LMS career).

Butlin's historian, Roger Billington, was a redcoat at Minehead in the 1960s, and he remembers kids climbing all over *Duchess of Hamilton*, imagining themselves on a train of seventeen coaches over Shap, perhaps – or maybe just treating the locomotive as a giant climbing frame.

Billington remembers Butlin fondly. 'He was probably the Richard Branson of his day,' he recalls. 'He wasn't an enthu-

RIGHT: The designer of the 'Duchesses', LMS Chief Mechanical Engineer William (later Sir) A. Stanier. National Railway Museum/SSPL

BELOW: As the first 'Duchess', 6220 *Coronation*, rolled out of Crewe Works, staff involved in her construction lined the tracks to see the finished article. Daily Herald Archive/NMeM/SSPL

RIGHT: The clean streamlining of *Coronation* was smoothly rounded like many modern trains. Viewed side-on before departure on its press debut, it lost much of its bulk.

Milepost 92¹/₂/railphotolibrary.com

LEFT: Assembling the streamlined casing on a 'Duchess' was a complex task, as was putting the finishing touches of gold 'speed whiskers' on the body.

Hulton-Deutsch Collection/Corbis

ABOVE: **6229** *Duchess of Hamilton* went to the USA in 1939, disguised as *Coronation*. Her streamlining was much smoother than her American counterparts.

Getty Images

LEFT: The record-breaking *Duchess of Abercorn* in her original form without smoke deflecting plates. This is how the unstreamlined 'Duchesses' looked before the war.

Milepost 92½/railphotolibrary.com

ABOVE: Though considered bulky by some, the streamlined 'Duchesses' had an imposing presence at speed, and looked surprisingly modern – a stark contrast with the now outdated infrastructure.

National Railway Museum/SSPL

RIGHT: The penultimate 'Duchess', 46256 *Sir William A. Stanier, F.R.S.*, built to compete with two prototype diesels ordered by the LMS. The cab sidesheets and pony truck are the most notable outward differences.

National Railway Museum/SSPL

LEFT: *Coronation* after arrival at Euston with the 114mph record-setting 'Coronation Scot' on June 29 1937.

Milepost 92½/railphotolibrary.com

RIGHT: *Duchess of Hamilton* was one of the stars of the main line in the 1980s and 90s, setting several power records. On October 26 1990, she hauls the 'Cumbrian Mountain Express' from Carlisle to Hellifield.

RIGHT: 'Duchesses' Hamilton and Sutherland were rescued by Billy Butlin for display at holiday camps. *Duchess of Sutherland* went to Ayr, while *Duchess of Hamilton* rested for a few years at Minehead, in the company of a 'Terrier' tank engine, as pictured here.

BELOW: The founder of Bloom's of Bressingham, Alan Bloom (in hat and overalls on the blue narrow-gauge engine) bought *Duchess of Sutherland* from Butlin's camp at Ayr. Bloom was passionate about steam, and was instrumental in the early days of railway preservation.

LEFT: *City of Birmingham* moved by road to its new home at Thinktank, Birmingham, in 2001, from the old Museum of Science and Industry. Special road trailers are needed to transport such huge locomotives.

Thinktank Trust

RIGHT: Size, presence, and power. The driving wheels of *City of Birmingham* alone are almost seven feet in diameter. Thinktank Trust

LEFT: The cabs of the 'Duchesses' were Spartan affairs. Beyond the half-open firehole doors of *City of Birmingham* is a firegrate with an area of fifty square feet – enough to beat some firemen.

Thinktank Trust

ABOVE: The quintessential image of a 'Duchess' — pounding up Shap with a long train.

National Railway Museum/SSPL

RIGHT: *Duchess of Sutherland* poses outside her base at Swanwick Junction with some of the people responsible for her overhaul.

J.B. Radford, John Stiles, PRCLT Collection

RIGHT: Brell Ewart of the Princess Royal Class Locomotive Trust presents HM The Queen with a ceremonial headlamp after *Duchess of Sutherland* hauled the Royal Train in 2002.
PA Photos

ABOVE: Three years later, 'Sutherland' was asked to haul the Royal Train again, this time over the Settle & Carlisle line – scene of *Duchess of Hamilton's* Blue Riband triumphs. On its way north, the train crosses the iconic Ribblehead Viaduct. PA Photos

LEFT: The Prince of Wales took the opportunity for a short cab ride in *Duchess of Sutherland*, but declined an invitation to have a go at firing the locomotive – perhaps he'd been briefed on the size of the grate...
Topfoto

BELOW: The Friends of the National Railway Museum commissioned a painting of *Duchess of Hamilton* being overhauled to raise funds for its operation. It provides a vivid illustration of the atmosphere of a railway workshop. National Railway Museum/SSPL

ABOVE: Even in 4mm to 1 foot scale, the 'Duchesses' have a presence like nothing else. Hornby's superb model lets old and young recreate the days when *City of Bristol* and her ilk dominated the West Coast rails and when diesels and electrics were few and far between. By kind permission of Hornby

siast, but he was always trying to get something different into his camps to differentiate them from the competition. It was a commercial decision to bring the locomotives in, but kids loved him for it – he got involved with things and made them happen: that's the sort of guy he was.'

The locomotives were invariably moved to the camps by rail as Butlin was shrewd enough to place his camps within easy reach of public transport, though some road movement was invariably necessary, particularly at Ayr, where the station that served the camp was on an embankment from where not even a temporary siding could be laid. Make no mistake, though – once the locomotives were safely ensconced in the camps, they proved a huge draw for holidaymakers, with thousands seeing the view from the footplate, and, on occasion, retired locomotive crew explaining how they worked.

At the time, the acquisition of big passenger locomotives was a very unusual thing to do – *Princess Elizabeth* had been saved by a dedicated group, and the industrialist Alan Pegler had bought *Flying Scotsman* in 1963, but even so, the scope of Butlin's purchases was in a different league altogether. For the time being, at least, four of the most important locomotives in Britain had been saved from the scrapman, and for that we must thank Walker, Ogg and of course Sir Billy himself, for their foresight, vision and persistence.

Chapter Sixteen
Brum Deal

I f Butlin's acquisitions of its two 'Duchesses' were the rapid-fire decisions of a company at the peak of its powers, the salvation of No. 46235 *City of Birmingham* was a much more considered affair that had its origins in the early 1950s, before withdrawal of the 'Duchesses' was even being considered. Birmingham Museum of Science & Industry opened its doors in 1951, and it was an ambitious undertaking for the time, the first really large industrial museum outside London. Its aim was to conserve significant machinery and artefacts from the industries of the West Midlands before they disappeared for ever. There was massive change in industry as well as the railways, and new production techniques and machinery were replacing steam-driven machines and traditional techniques that had dominated the West Midlands manufacturing sector for decades – the museum's mission was nothing less than to preserve as much material as possible for future generations.

The first director of the museum was Norman Birtenshaw, and he was something of a visionary, rapidly increasing the collection of stationary steam engines, and, from 1954, of transport. Birmingham had a big railway industry, but unlike Crewe, it concentrated on building carriages and wagons. Birtenshaw, however, wanted a steam locomotive for the transport collection, and started considering what would make an appropriate exhibit. He had to bear in mind the future impact such an exhibit would have on visitors, while ensuring there was a connection with Birmingham. It was a tough challenge, as the locomotives that typically operated into the city tended to be second-line types such as the 'Royal Scots' and 'Jubilees', as trains from Birmingham to London obviously had much shorter journeys than the Anglo-Scottish expresses, and tended to be shorter too.

In 1953 he contacted the curator of the British Transport Museum, then in Clapham, London, for suggestions and to see whether his museum would represent a suitable home for a big steam locomotive. With approval gained, he decided to go for No. 46235 *City of Birmingham*, largely because of its name but also because the 'Duchesses' represented the peak of steam's power and size: there was no question of whether it would make an impressive exhibit! In 1956 Birtenshaw expressed interest in the locomotive to the London Midland Region, and in 1959 detailed negotiations were started with the chairman of the British Transport Commission, Sir Brian Robertson, to reserve the locomotive.

Key to the negotiations was when *City of Birmingham* would be available, and 1960 threw up a surprising – and for Birmingham, welcome – result. The locomotive, the railway said, wouldn't be available for another ten years. This was good for Birmingham Museum of Science & Industry as it would have to build an extension in order to accommodate such a large exhibit, but it remains an intriguing remark. As Jack Kirkby, the Collections Interpretations Manager of

Thinktank, the museum's modern-day successor, says, it could have been a glib off-the-cuff remark intended to give the London Midland Region flexibility in when it disposed of the locomotive. But he also says that it could have represented a more solid idea at the time of how long the 'Duchesses' would be in service. I've never read of such a plan anywhere else, so it's unlikely to be official, but this remarkable assertion, contained in a letter to the museum from the London Midland Region, suggests that at an unofficial but fairly high level, it was thought the 'Duchesses' would be replaced like-for-like by electric locomotives, skipping the diesel stage altogether. In 1960 at least, it seems it was expected the 'Duchesses' would be in service rather longer than they were.

After No. 46235 was withdrawn in October 1964, she was stored at Crewe for a while, before moving to Nuneaton for storage in January 1965. In October that year, she moved to Crewe for further storage before cosmetic overhaul. That didn't happen until March the following year, when *City of Birmingham* was admitted to the paint shop for cosmetic overhaul. She wouldn't emerge until May 1966. Jack Kirkby calls this a 'suspiciously long time' and, to this day, nobody has been able to explain precisely why it took so long. The simplest and most likely explanation is that work was undertaken on the locomotive during quiet periods – after all, the paint shop would have been busy on revenue-earning locomotives – but there is one other possibility that Kirkby doesn't reject out of hand either: that the locomotive was given a much more thorough overhaul in secret by Crewe.

There is form for this. No. 4073 *Caerphilly Castle* was

earmarked for preservation by the Science Museum, London, and was given a cosmetic overhaul at Swindon. When she moved to Steam – the Museum of the Great Western Railway, in Swindon, a few years ago, one of the enthusiast magazines interviewed volunteers and staff there, and was greeted by the stunning assertion that 'She's a fresh off!' – in other words, a complete heavy general overhaul had been performed on the locomotive even though she would never steam again. If that's true, one could almost simply light a fire, fill the boiler and drive off with a locomotive still essentially fresh from the Swindon Works production line.

Could something similar have happened with *City of Birmingham*? It's possible. There would have been enough of the consumable parts such as boiler tubes in store for replacement to be made, and at a time when parts for steam locomotives had no more than scrap value, their use may not even have been noticed. The men tasked with overhauling her would have known that this might be their last chance to demonstrate their craftsmanship for posterity – and decided to do as much work as they could unofficially. Certainly that's the case for the cosmetic aspects of the restoration, which are now just about the last surviving original examples of British Railways paint, and it might just have happened with the mechanicals too. Kirkby says it's entirely possible, but the only way of knowing would be to dismantle the locomotive and investigate thoroughly – and given that one would have to dismantle large parts of Thinktank, that's not likely to happen soon, if ever.

After cosmetic restoration, *City of Birmingham* was moved

first to Saltley depot, just outside Birmingham, and then to Lawley Street, the container terminal one can see on the eastern approaches to New Street station. From there, the locomotive was moved by road to the museum, causing absolute chaos in the city centre as roads had to be closed while the locomotive was gently and slowly moved to her new home. The problem was that her new home wasn't ready. After arrival on 22 May 1966, a temporary structure was put around the locomotive while the locomotive hall was literally built around her.

The official presentation to Birmingham City Council by British Rail was made in July 1966 by E.R. Williams, the divisional manager for the area. In his speech, he said:

> The presentation of this locomotive to the city is an indication of the close links which bind Birmingham and the railways who played a central part in the growth and development of the city during the past century.
>
> It is fitting that this fine example of the steam locomotives now disappearing from the scene should find a resting place in the museum at a time when electric traction will soon make its impact on Birmingham.

Like many government projects, the locomotive hall opened late, and it wasn't until 1972 that *City of Birmingham* was under cover in a purpose-built structure, and able to move slowly for a few metres via an electro-hydraulic ram. Birtenshaw's vision meant that when hasty decisions had to be made about which steam locomotives were to be saved for the National Collection in the 1960s, there was no need to worry about finding a location for a 'Duchess' as one already had a permanent home earmarked for her.

As the 1960s progressed, the decline of steam became an ever more sorry spectacle. The Southern Region finally withdrew its last steam locomotives in 1967, leaving an ever-shrinking number of depots in the north-west to hold the candle. The end finally came on 11 August 1968, with the famous 'Fifteen Guinea Special', hauled by 'Black 5s' in part and the last operating 'Britannia', 70013 *Oliver Cromwell*. And then it was all over — or was it?

Chapter Seventeen
Brave New World

Even as the last fires were being dropped on British Railways' last steam locomotives, moves were afoot to secure an operating future for steam elsewhere in Britain. The 1953 film *The Titfield Thunderbolt* poked gentle fun at the idea of locals taking over their local line, which had been closed by BR, but this Ealing comedy was to prove eerily prophetic about what the future held for some railways – and it was mostly thanks to Dr Beeching himself.

The so-called 'Beeching Cuts' of the 1960s (actually, Beeching had departed when many of the lines were closed) eliminated a third of the rail network in a bid to save money. Many of the lines closed were branch lines, though some, such as the Great Central from London Marylebone to Leicester and Nottingham, and the old Southern Railway route from Plymouth to Exeter, were main lines too. Such was the pace of closure that many lines were left to rot, often for years, before the demolition gangs moved in. And for many rail enthusiasts, the temptation to see trains running on them again was too much to resist.

In the early 1950s, preservation got going on narrow-gauge railways in Wales, and it wasn't long before enthusiasts turned their attention to standard-gauge railways, which hitherto had seemed too daunting to take on. The

Middleton Railway in Leeds and the Bluebell Railway in East Sussex were both taken over by volunteer organisations, in 1959 and 1960 respectively, and they formed the vanguard of the standard-gauge preservation movement.

It took a little while for things to get going elsewhere, but, as the success of the first two lines grew, other groups formed in a bid to save railways in their part of the world. The Keighley & Worth Valley Railway in West Yorkshire started in June 1968, and other lines, such as the North Yorkshire Moors Railway, Severn Valley Railway and Paignton & Dartmouth Steam Railway had also or were soon to start running.

Initially they tended to operate using small engines, either bought from BR, or from industry, which used huge numbers of locomotives at the time. Some tried to operate regular services in a bid to totally reverse their line's closure, but surprisingly quickly reverted to operating steam trains for the sake of operating steam trains, and an initially sceptical public gradually warmed to the idea of volunteers running their own trains.

Getting hold of locomotives was a particular problem in those early days. While they could be and were bought from BR, inevitably as steam was eliminated it got more difficult to acquire good examples. And the preservation movement needed to have locomotives that wouldn't take much, or better still, any, work to get operational as the volunteers simply didn't have the equipment or expertise to undertake major repairs. By the end of the 1960s, if it hadn't been for one scrap merchant in Wales, the chances are that the locomotives saved by 1968, plus some industrials saved in the following decade, would have been the entire steam fleet.

Sometimes, though, fate plays a favourable hand, and when the scrap merchant Dai Woodham decided to stop cutting up the steam locomotives at his yard in Barry, Wales, in favour of more easily dismantled material such as carriages and wagons, the die was cast for railway preservation to build up a head of steam. There were something like 200 steam locomotives at Barry Scrapyard, and most of them were from the London Midland, Western and Southern Regions, including No. 71000 *Duke of Gloucester* (the one-off successor to No. 46202 *Princess Anne*, which was wrecked in the Harrow accident), and many were steamable without too much work. By the end of the 1960s, the procession of locomotives into Barry Scrapyard had been reversed, as various groups raised money to buy and then restore their chosen engines.

The pictures of the time show an incongruous sight. There were line after line after line of rusting steam locomotives. It looked like an old shed yard that had been abandoned and left to decay – and it didn't take long for word to get out. Initially enthusiasts came to reminisce and reacquaint themselves with steam, but that soon transformed into a desire to get engines running. The first locomotive left the yard in September 1968, a month after steam had ended on British Rail, and others followed over the next twenty years or so.

Woodham wasn't an enthusiast himself, but he did what he could to help groups who wanted to buy the locomotives. Eventually, almost all the locomotives were rescued for preservation, forming the heart of today's steam fleet. Woodham, who was awarded the MBE for his business initiatives in South Wales, died in 1994, an unlikely ally of railway preservation, but one whose place in history is well deserved.

British Rail had been determined for a long time that, once steam was finished, that was it, and *Flying Scotsman* was only able to operate through the 1960s because of a comprehensive and watertight agreement that her owner, Alan Pegler, had sealed when he bought the locomotive. After 1968, if you wanted to see a steam locomotive, you had to go to one of the preserved railways, or seek out the dwindling number of industrial sites that still used steam.

Chapter Eighteen
Blooming Marvellous!

The sudden growth of railway preservation came at an opportune time for Butlin's two 'Duchesses'. The 1960s are always heralded as a decade of great change, and that included the expectations of holidaymakers. Butlin's was always very good at keeping its resorts fresh and interesting, and by the end of the 1960s, people were looking to the future rather than the past. Many children had never seen a steam locomotive in action before, and were naturally far more interested in other things, such as cars and aeroplanes. The two 'Duchesses' were rather out of keeping with the spirit of the age. Their presence at Minehead and Ayr hadn't escaped the attentions of rail enthusiasts, who were starting to get worried about their long-term future. The salty sea air is notoriously corrosive, and all of Butlin's locomotives were showing signs of weathering. By now they had outlived their usefulness as attractions, and the company was open to suggestions to release them.

The opening moves were made by Geoffrey Sands, a former area manager for British Railways, now on the staff at Blooms of Bressingham, Norfolk. In charge of Bressingham was one of the leading lights of railway preservation, Alan Bloom. Bloom was a steam enthusiast through and through, and had built up an enviable collection of traction engines. He had also provided a home from home for the

National Collection's 70013 *Oliver Cromwell*, which was one of the stars of 1968. Sands visited Skegness in 1970 and saw the state of *Royal Scot* – and immediately decided to persuade Bloom to get it to Bressingham. 'I'd dearly love to see it here,' he told his boss. 'The man in charge of Skegness says it's a nuisance standing there rusting away with people tampering with it – an eyesore rather than an attraction.'

Alan Bloom is a legend in railway preservation and beyond, thanks to his nursery, Blooms of Bressingham, at Diss, near Thetford, Norfolk. Bloom was born in 1906 into a family that owned a nursery in Cambridgeshire. After a lengthy and varied apprenticeship, he started his own business in 1926, which soon became highly successful. After the war, he set up a new nursery on 228 acres of land at Bressingham, and, by 1955, when he returned to Britain after a few unsuccessful years in Canada, his new nursery was said to be the largest producer of hardy perennials in Britain. With his long hair (which *The Times* in his obituary described accurately as 'leonine') and forthright character, he was a great showman.

Bloom had already made one approach, in 1968, which Butlin's rejected, but he tried again, reminding the holiday camp company that Bressingham had engineers and facilities where *Royal Scot* could be looked after. The letter prompted Butlin's to re-evaluate its steam locomotives and it decided to release them all as they would soon require significant expenditure, which Butlin's couldn't justify.

A Butlin's director visited Bressingham, and agreed that if Bloom paid for all transport and restoration costs – and kept them in good condition – he could have them on permanent loan. Six locomotives would have been too many, especially the four large ones, and Bloom made the availability of the locomotives known to other preservation groups. The way was set for Bressingham to acquire four, but they reckoned without the deadlines imposed by Butlin's brochure printers. It turned out that *Duchess of Hamilton* and *Princess Margaret Rose* had been promised on display at Minehead and Pwllheli for the 1971 season, and Butlin's couldn't risk breaching the Trades Description Act. Those two loco-motives would have to wait, but agreement was reached for *Duchess of Sutherland*, *Royal Scot*, 32662 *Martello* and 30102 *Granville* (the latter two were small tank engines) to go to Bressingham on permanent loan.

Duchess of Sutherland was the first locomotive to be moved, on 1 March 1971, and after being taken by road from the holiday camp to Ayr Townhead coal yard, was set to make her journey south by rail. When she'd arrived at the camp back in 1964, the shedmaster at Newton-on-Ayr depot, William Bennett, had ensured that every moving part was well greased and lubricated to prevent them from seizing up, and, as the locomotive was pulled onto the low-loader, his actions were proved: the locomotive was hauled smoothly and easily onto the trailer. Some work beforehand was needed to ensure brake systems, the regulator, reverser, and, of course, the motion, still functioned, but generally, little work was needed to make a locomotive that had been stored outside for almost seven years fit for being hauled.

It was loaded onto the British Rail network at Townhead yard, before being hauled south to Thetford by rail. It would be a tricky and long movement for all concerned. The locomotive was not allowed to be hauled at more than 25mph, and regular checks had to be made on all wheel bearings to ensure that they weren't seizing up. Normally the valve gear was taken off for this sort of movement as years of storage meant it was much more likely to seize, but in this case, it was left on with no ill effects. The journey took twenty-eight hours and, according to David Ward, the London Midland Region's passenger marketing director, 'did her a power of good, and she now runs like a sewing machine.' Ward was referring to the locomotive's freedom of movement, and there's no doubt that this boded well for the forthcoming restoration at Bressingham. Bill Harvey, who accompanied the locomotive on her way south, and who had until recently run BR's maintenance depot at Norwich, startled a Norwich shopkeeper by asking for 'a pint of castor oil for the "Duchess", please,' in the weeks before the movement, according to the *Eastern Daily Express*. The reason was simple: Harvey reckoned that castor oil was the best thing for lubricating bearings that might easily seize up.

Even while *Duchess of Sutherland* was on her way south, preservationists disgruntled at the wholesale acquisition of Butlin's locomotives by Bressingham mounted a legal challenge. Led by Dr Peter Beet, the owner of a number of locomotives based at Carnforth, the decision on where No. 46233's new home should be should have been based on a postal ballot organised by the Transport Trust, the body invited to make recommendations on the new homes for the Butlin's locomotives. Beet issued a writ against the Transport Trust, though Butlin's was understandably nonplussed as it couldn't see why someone else should decide what happened to its property. Though the challenge was withdrawn in March 1971, Butlin's decided to delay decisions on where the other locomotives should go until it had considered it properly. It wouldn't be until 1975 that No. 46229 *Duchess of Hamilton* would leave Minehead.

With *Duchess of Sutherland* safe at Bressingham, Alan Bloom and the team there wasted little time in starting to restore her to working order. Bressingham has always placed much emphasis on having working steam, and back in those days before health and safety rules prevented us from having more than a moderate and approved amount of fun, was able to offer footplate rides on its short running line.

Investigations into *Duchess of Sutherland*'s condition began in 1972 in order to ascertain what and how much work it would take to restore her. Generally, she was found to be in surprisingly good condition considering her years out in the open at Ayr. The firebox needed some work, and the small boiler tubes were replaced. Other aspects of the boiler, such as superheater tubes, were repaired or replaced as necessary.

The smokebox door ring, which surrounds the door, was heavily corroded and large parts had to be replaced, and some of the external cladding was also in poor condition. Inevitably there were smaller parts that needed replacement that could only be discovered when work started. Brell Ewart and Brian Radford wrote in *6233 Duchess of Sutherland and the Princess Coronation Class* (the definitive source on the locomotive) that a small die nut needed to ensure the small tubes fitted snugly at the firebox end of the boiler had to be made specially, at a cost of £47 – a large amount of money then, and one for something that only weighed four ounces!

Bloom had badly underestimated the work needed to restore No. 6100 *Royal Scot* to working order, the work coming in at more than £10,000 against initial estimates of £3,000, but he wasn't about to skimp on the 'Duchess'. One area that proved predictably problematic was cleaning rust from exterior surfaces. On the outside of the locomotive, this is fairly easy, but on the underside and on the areas between the frames, it is a lengthy and laborious process, especially on an engine the size of *Duchess of Sutherland*. 'Someone suggested sand-blasting,' he wrote in *The Railway Magazine*. 'What it would cost by hand over a period of months could be done by blasting in a few days at no greater cost, so we were told.'

The optimism was badly misplaced as contractors covered large areas of the restoration shed with sand ankle-deep in places despite a protective cocoon being placed around the locomotive. After the contractors left, painting of the apparently clean surfaces began, and it quickly became clear that the multitude of nooks and crannies on the locomotive had been left unscathed by the sand-blasters. There was nothing for it – someone had to go underneath and finish the job by hand.

It took a long time, but gradually the locomotive took shape and Bob Rolfe, the man who painted *Royal Scot* at Bressingham, was tasked with painting No. 6233. He applied four undercoats, then the top coat, and finally the lettering and lining out, the latter using real gold leaf. The painting and gilding cost more than £500, but having already spent £16,000 on restoring the engine, Bloom felt this final expense to get it right was worth it. He estimated more than

20,000 man-hours had been spent on restoration over the two years.

On 28 May 1974, after more than a decade of silence, the fire was lit once more in *Duchess of Sutherland*, and two days later she was giving cab-rides to visitors. At last, people could enjoy the spectacle of one of these giant locomotives running again. It might only be for a short distance, but it represented a huge achievement for Bloom, Bressingham, and for *Duchess of Sutherland* herself. That Thursday, *Duchess of Sutherland* was officially launched by the Countess of Sutherland, marking the completion of a remarkable and at times unlikely resurrection.

Sadly it didn't last long, as the firebox tubeplate started to develop a leak in 1976. Sometimes leaks appear that seal themselves when a boiler gets warm, but they can never be ignored for long. Investigations suggested the only solution was a new firebox tubeplate, and the estimated cost of £12,000 was too much for Bressingham to justify. It was no criticism of the restoration work carried out by Bressingham as with any restored machine, it's impossible to identify all the potential faults until you actually start running it. One must also remember that, although Bressingham's engineering facilities were very good, they weren't Crewe Works, and repair techniques possible today simply hadn't been developed by then. From 1976, *Duchess of Sutherland* was to remain a popular static exhibit at Bressingham.

Bloom was always sensitive to critics who felt the locomotives at Bressingham should be steamed, particularly those who wanted *Duchess of Sutherland* back in action. In a withering reply to one such call in the pages of *Steam Railway*, he wrote: 'The correspondent betrays the selfish ignorance of the gricing [rail enthusiast] fraternity. Their fanaticism begins and ends with steam-hauled trains and they are quite oblivious to the vastly greater numbers who have a more open nostalgia for steam in preservation. Many people lack the opportunity or inclination to travel on steam-hauled trains or to spend hours at the lineside.'

He continued: 'Are [the correspondent] and his like so selfish and one-track minded as to wish to deny [ordinary visitors to Bressingham] the sight of express locomotives in an unusual setting? Both No. 6100 *Royal Scot* and No. 6233 *Duchess of Sutherland* have been used at Bressingham for footplate rides and will, we hope, serve that same purpose again in the future. It is by no means a dishonourable form of active retirement when it provides so much interest for so many who would otherwise be denied the experience of steam power, whether nostalgic, or educational or both.'

It was a response from Bloom that set out the stall for definite: *Duchess of Sutherland* would stay at Bressingham and would not run on the main line. But by then it didn't matter, as moves were already afoot to get another 'Duchess' steaming.

Chapter Nineteen
Duchess of York

Peter Beet's aborted legal challenge against Bressingham's acquisition of the entire Butlin's steam locomotive fleet eventually meant that the two remaining locomotives, No. 46203 *Princess Margaret Rose* and No. 6229 *Duchess of Hamilton*, wouldn't make the trip to Norfolk (something of a blessing for Bressingham as space would have been very tight if they had arrived). Butlin's was keen to see the locomotives depart, however, and offered *Princess Margaret Rose* to the Midland Railway Centre. *Duchess of Hamilton*, however, was to go to one of the most high-profile preservation establishments in the world, the newly opened National Railway Museum in York.

In February 1975, a twenty-year loan was agreed with the Museum, which opened to the public in autumn that year, but before *Duchess of Hamilton* could be placed on display, she needed fettling up after years in the sea air at Minehead. The Norton Fitzwarren (near Taunton) to Minehead branch had been closed by British Rail but was still intact, and after investigation, it was decided to send a diesel locomotive over the line to take *Duchess of Hamilton* to BR's Swindon Works, where she would be cosmetically restored to as-withdrawn conditions, due to her rounded smokebox – BR Crimson Lake with LMS lining and numbered No. 46229. That line, incidentally, is now the very successful West Somerset Railway.

She arrived at Swindon after a low-speed journey rather similar to that of *Duchess of Sutherland* a couple of years before and then spent a year undergoing cosmetic restoration to restore her appearance to that of a newly overhauled loco-motive and put right the corrosion incurred at Minehead. Although Swindon wasn't, perhaps, the busiest of railway works at the time, there were still plenty of other tasks to keep its staff occupied, but given the inevitable travails of opening the new museum in York, there was no hurry for her to arrive, and it wasn't until early 1976 that she took her place in the museum's Great Hall.

She was formally unveiled on 26 May that year and took centre stage at the museum, and it wasn't long before thoughts started turning to overhauling her for use on the main line. Although BR had axed steam in 1968, cracks soon started appearing in its nominally steam-proof façade, and after a pioneering run using No. 6000 *King George V* in 1971, steam locomotives gradually began to venture out onto the main line at the head of enthusiasts' specials. This was the ambition for *Duchess of Hamilton*.

One of the driving forces behind the overhaul of *Duchess of Hamilton* was David Jenkinson (who sadly died in 2004), then working at the NRM as head of education and research, and one of the leading authorities on the LMS. He was one of the founders of the LMS Society, and a devout admirer of the 'Duchesses'. Jenkinson found ready support at the museum to return *Duchess of Hamilton* to operational condition, and from May 1978 to 1980 the locomotive was overhauled after an extensive fundraising campaign that included the commissioning of a painting of the locomotive by the legendary railway artist Terence Cuneo. It was funded by the Friends of the National Railway Museum, an independent supporting organisation founded the year before to help conserve and operate exhibits that might not otherwise receive attention and funding, and the Friends' Chief Mechanical Engineer, John Peck, was to oversee the overhaul. Two experienced engineers, Kim Malyon and Peter Pickering, were employed by the Friends to maintain the locomotive.

Initial investigations suggested that a boiler lift wouldn't be needed to refurbish the parts underneath. As soon as a boiler lift is involved – which, as the term suggests, means you have to remove the boiler from the rest of the locomotive – overhauls become much more complicated, but although this was avoided, there was still a lot of work to do. All the small tubes in the boiler needed replacement, and the main steam pipe needed repairing too because it had split. Bit by bit the various niggling faults were cured. Parts were borrowed from *Duchess of Sutherland*, now out of steam at Bressingham, while others were borrowed from locomotives at York.

Eventually, on 14 April, the boiler was steamed, and after a few of the inevitable glitches were repaired, *Duchess of Hamilton* was ready to make her main-line debut from York on a circular itinerary via Leeds and Harrogate on 10 May. The anticipation amongst enthusiasts to see the 'Duchess' running was immense. Not since No. 46256 *Sir William A. Stanier, F.R.S.* had hauled portions of the 'Scottish

Lowlander' railtour back in 1964 had a 'Duchess' hauled a train, and now not only was *Duchess of Hamilton* going to do it, she was going to do so on the main line.

The weather seemed to bless the day, shining bright and warm, a relief to the people who'd come to see the debut of the 'Duchess'. The driver, Arthur Fussy, was careful with his new steed, and her performance was rather sedate by the sort of standards she was used to, but even so, she needed little encouragement to creep above the 60mph blanket speed limit imposed by BR on steam locomotives. The journalist David Wilcock was on this train, and he wrote: 'I think it was around Church Fenton that I smelt it. I stuck my head out of the starboard side for a view down the length of that shimmering maroon body when I caught the waft of vapour . . .

'. . . it was pure, unadulterated Camden. Not Willesden or Cricklewood or Kentish Town, but that undeniable sheddy smell that was once London North West One . . .'

Wilcock for a moment, like many others, was lost in time, and though he was sorry that – at the time – it seemed unlikely a 'Duchess' would ever return to Shap, the fact that it was possible to travel behind one once more was enough. The 'Duchess' was back.

Very quickly *Duchess of Hamilton* became accustomed to the more restricted routes she was allowed to operate on, most being in the north of England on routes with spare capacity. It was difficult, given the 60mph restriction, to really push the locomotive, but on 1 November 1980 she headed to a line that in time she would almost make her own: the Settle–Carlisle line (S&C). It is one of the most scenic railways in Britain, the last main line built with pick and shovel, and it allowed the Midland Railway its own route to Scotland, but the scenic beauty of the line contrasts harshly with the steep gradients. The likes of Ais Gill are not as well known as Shap, but they have entered folklore amongst railwaymen.

Duchess of Hamilton's debut run did not cover her in glory. Slippery track caused by wet leaves landing on the rails and being pulped to a substance as slippery as ice (yes, it was a problem back then too!) meant she slipped to a standstill twice at the head of her thirteen-coach train. She first slipped at Bell Busk, midway between Skipton and Hellifield, but recovered well from a stand and hit 60mph at Settle Junction. The good running wouldn't last – just past the station she slipped again and had to be rescued by a diesel. It wasn't the locomotive's fault – not only do most big 'Pacifics' slip easily unless expertly handled at the best of times, conditions on the rails were so bad that for a while all freight trains on the line were provided with extra assistance in case of slipping – but it wasn't an auspicious start to her career.

Said Kim Malyon afterwards, 'The rail conditions were bad, there's no doubt about that, and it was true that two coaches had their brakes dragging, but the fact was that the sanders didn't work at a time when we most needed them . . . it was really down to bad preparation and everyone was blaming everyone else – all very embarrassing.'

Her main-line career took off from then. She soon became one of the stars of the steam railway movement, and on 23 May 1981 hauled the first 'Scarborough Spa Express', a series of semi-regular steam-hauled trains from York to the seaside resort.

The levels of performance of main-line steam are largely dictated by today's changed railway environment and the rigid and constraining framework of rules within which they have to operate. The train timing and performance expert Mike Notley was present on many of *Duchess of Hamilton*'s main-line runs in the 1980s and 1990s. His take on main-line steam operation reflects the changed operating circumstances *Duchess of Hamilton* now found herself in.

In their prime the 'Duchesses' were 'cock of the roost' and responsible for the daily working of trains which took priority over everything else. Preserved main-line steam is a very different matter, coming way down the pecking order and providing far fewer opportunities for them to perform as they were intended to.

Opportunities for sustained running on the true main lines are limited by restraints on maximum speed, clearance and weight restrictions and the problems of simply fitting in with today's faster, more intensive service on a railway that has lost much of the flexibility it had in steam's heyday. But when those chances have presented themselves, they have largely been eagerly grasped and the 'Duchesses', as should be expected, have been in the forefront of things and producing performances, not just of outstanding quality but of historical significance.

The 'Duchesses' were built for speed and power and both *Hamilton* and *Sutherland* have been prevented from exploiting the first of these qualities by arbitrary speed ceilings. 46229 was affected even more than 6233 for, throughout her two spells on the main line, she was officially limited to 60mph. I say 'officially' limited because there were occasions when the limit was, shall we say, very liberally interpreted, as those who were lucky enough to be on the trains involved will well know.

But while *Duchess of Hamilton* was artificially restrained in the realms of speed, there was nothing the authorities could do when it came to power – and this was how *Duchess of Hamilton* built her reputation. During her first spell back on the main line between 1980 and 1985, steam was operated on a very limited number of secondary routes. The flattish nature of the North Wales Coast route offered no real opportunity for a 'Duchess' to unleash her power and while the Welsh Marches line from Shrewsbury to Newport, Wales, offered at least some token challenges, it was the Settle–Carlisle line with its north and southbound climbs to Ais Gill that provided the main arena for No. 46229 to demonstrate her might.

In the early 1980s many of the trains the 'Duchess' hauled were formed of the old Steam Locomotive Operators Association (SLOA) Pullman cars, which were heavy vehicles and with a limited carrying capacity. So, to maximise seating capacity, trains were regularly loaded to thirteen vehicles, and even fourteen of these heavy cars generated little concern. As trains were heavy, on the long 1-in-100 gradients, sustained power was the order of the day. And No. 46229 had more than anything else.

'In the early 1980s,' says Notley, '*Duchess of Hamilton*

simply had the field to herself and a rivalry developed between some of the Carlisle crews to see who could cover the southbound climb to Ais Gill summit fastest. The time was taken between Mileposts 275 and 259¾ and the marker seems to have been set down on March 19 1983 when 46229, hauling a train of 560 tons, posted a time of 19 min 31 sec for the 15¼ miles. A couple of months later, with a similar load, this was reduced by six seconds. And then, on January 7 1984, with a lighter train of 485 tons, Driver Willie Alexander and Fireman Paul Kane reduced this to an outstanding time of 17 min 57 secs, passing the summit at 53mph.'

This set a record, and set the scene for some memorable events a few years later. In the meantime, *Duchess of Hamilton* was involved in working a series of trains between Marylebone and Stratford-upon-Avon that took her up the relatively innocuous gradients of Saunderton Bank. After her exertions on the S&C, gradients of 1-in-164/179 would hardly seem to merit her attention but, on 26 May 1985 in the hands of Driver Read, she wrote a new page in the history book of British steam. Perhaps with impending withdrawal as the spur, No. 6229 accelerated a 430-ton gross trailing weight from a dead stand at High Wycombe to 75mph at Milepost 22¼, about a mile north of Saunderton.

Notley did his calculations, and reckons that power peaked at 3,560hp for over 3½ minutes, a record for a British steam locomotive that still stands to this day. And as if to prove that this was no fluke, she almost repeated the feat with an average of 3,460hp before her withdrawal in October 1985.

This was an incredible performance, beating even *Duchess of Abercorn* in 1939 — though as there was no test car in the train, it isn't counted as an official record. And this time the only locomotives in Britain that could beat that horsepower figure were electrics: *Duchess of Hamilton* had proved that even twenty-one years after she was withdrawn, she could not just beat, but utterly overwhelm even the most powerful diesels.

Duchess of Hamilton bowed out of main-line service on 26 October 1985, after hauling another 'Cumbrian Mountain Express'. She had covered thousands of miles, and passed the 1.5 million milestone since she was built, and John Peck had realised that she hadn't received a comprehensive heavy overhaul since October 1959, more than twenty-five years before. It was time, he said, 'to give her the cure'. That the locomotive needed it was beyond doubt. Various leaks and knocks had made themselves apparent, and this time it wouldn't be possible to overhaul her without lifting the boiler and doing it comprehensively.

Kim Malyon, one of the men so heavily involved with the locomotive, reflected on the five years he had spent with her in *Steam Railway* back in 1985, and for him, it was something of an eye-opener. 'To me, an "A4" was the ultimate piece of machinery. Nobody could convince me that anything could beat an "A4" for out-and-out power — but I've had to change my mind. Mr Stanier's four-cylinder "Princess Coronation" can. We've had more than 3,000 horsepower from the ol' girl ploughing up the Settle & Carlisle — they never had that on Rugby Test Plant!'

Further problems were found, and it became clear that

the overhaul would be a long and painful one. I go into more detail about overhauling a steam locomotive later in the book, so I won't repeat it here, but Peck and his team had real concern about just how much metal was left after those years stored at Minehead. The tender was a particular cause for concern as it was badly wasted, so much so that it actually needed a new tank.

During this process, the NRM bought the locomotive from Butlin's as the holiday company was now actively seeking to remove the locomotives from its balance sheet. *Duchess of Hamilton* was now the museum's to do with as it pleased, and no short cuts were taken in the overhaul to working order. To all intents and purposes, she would be as good as new when she emerged from York. She returned to traffic on 29 March 1990, and, following a successful test run from Derby to Sheffield, she went back on the main line.

It had been good, and soon things would get even better.

Chapter Twenty

The Blue Riband

Other big 'Pacific' steam locomotives were pushed to try to beat *Duchess of Hamilton*'s times over the climb to Ais Gill, and an unofficial competition universally known as 'The Blue Riband' was established after *Duchess of Hamilton*'s performances in early 1983 by Kim Malyon, who ran a piece of blue ribbon from the smokebox to the bufferbeam. Cheekily, it was inscribed with the words 'To commemorate the most outstanding run by a preserved locomotive over the S&C'. It was something of a wind-up on Malyon's part, but the owners of other locomotives were more than up for a contest. Despite their best efforts, nothing could quite match the big red 'Duchess', not even the streamlined 'A4s' of the old LNER.

On her return to the main line in 1990, for the first time, *Duchess of Hamilton* found her position of supremacy challenged, initially by the unique BR Standard 'Pacific' No. 71000 *Duke of Gloucester* and then, further, by 'A2' No. 60532 *Blue Peter*. And it was the S&C that was to be the testing ground over which these giants pitted their strength.

The informal contest between loco crews of the early 1980s inspired by Malyon had now become a semi-official contest with the title of 'The Blue Riband'. And like any contest it had rules. The title was given to the locomotive recording the fastest time between Mileposts 275 and 259¾ hauling a trailing load of at least twelve coaches. As any more than twelve coaches imposed a significant handicap, it was the twelve-coach trains that battled it out.

The gauntlet was thrown down on 20 July 1991 when Driver Alexander and Fireman Kane bettered their time with the 'Duchess' by recording 17 minutes exactly with *Duke of Gloucester*. *Blue Peter* got close, recording 17 min 33 sec on 21 March 1992. Again the footplate crew was Alexander and Kane. Now it was *Duchess of Hamilton*'s turn – and Mike Notley was there.

Hamilton had a 'sighter' on April 24 1993, posting a time of 17 min 23 sec but it was still No. 71000 *Duke of Gloucester* that reigned supreme. That was until August 14 1993. As *Duchess of Hamilton* left Carlisle on a southbound 'Cumbrian Mountain Express' on a cool, dry day with little wind, she was in the hands of one of Carlisle's younger drivers, Brian Grierson. Paul Kane was firing and plans were afoot to do something about the 'Blue Riband'. I can do no better than quote the notes I made at the time:

Speed picked up down to Ormside, hitting 60mph – and then the fireworks began! As we entered Helm Tunnel we were doing 55mph and only dropped to 53½ at Griseburn. The 1¼ miles to Milepost 270½ saw an increase to 58, and the next two miles of easier gradients brought this up to 66mph.

Hamilton was going well, and pounded her way up the 1-in-100 to Birkett Tunnel, entering at 52½ and dropping to a minimum of 49½ at Milepost 264. The following mile saw a recovery to 55mph before the final three-mile pitch of 1-in-100 to Milepost 260. This saw a gradual fall to 52mph involving an average equivalent drawbar horsepower of around 2,500, an incredible feat, coming after just 17 minutes of hard steaming. The record looked on.

The final level quarter-mile to Milepost 259¾ (Ais Gill Summit) saw an acceleration to 54mph and, with whistle blasting triumphantly, we passed the summit in a new 'Blue Riband' record time of 16 minutes 14 seconds, an improvement of over three-quarters of a minute on the *Duke*'s previous record.

At Garsdale everyone wanted to know whether *Duchess of Hamilton* had broken the record. Jimmy MacLelland, the traction inspector, was smiling broadly and proudly displaying his stopwatch, which showed the time up from Milepost 275. Notley managed to get a word with Jimmy, who was exuberant, telling him that they had apparently done most of the climb on full regulator and 55% cut-off. Both injectors had been on the whole way and the steam pressure needle had been rock steady on 250psi.

Other crews with *Duke of Gloucester* got close, but *Duchess of Hamilton*'s record still stands.

By the mid-1990s, railway privatisation was looming, and there was unease across the whole railway. Almost every railway in the world owned the tracks and the trains, viewing the two as an integrated system, but Britain was to do things differently. The tracks, signals and all the infrastructure were to be owned by a stock market-listed company called Railtrack, while British Rail's passenger operations would be parcelled off into something like twenty-five separate franchises, which would be operated by the highest bidder. Track maintenance would also be privatised, with Railtrack having to use contractors instead of its own staff. It would prove a disastrous combination in view of accidents that would happen around the turn of the century.

Privatisation was viewed with real fear by the steam movement as concerns grew that main-line steam could be squeezed off the railway, but it became an unexpected beneficiary of the so-called 'open access' policy. The aim was to ensure competition on the railway by allowing anyone with the money and qualifications to run their own trains wherever they wanted, subject to the train itself being suitable for the route, and there being track space available. For steam, the niggling route restrictions of British Rail, even though they had gradually been extended, were over, and the mid-1990s saw a significant widening of the range of steam operations. No. 46229 was at last able to work over the route she had graced in her LMS/BR days, the West Coast Main Line.

She took part in the 'Shap Trials' in the autumn of 1995, a trial of strength between No. 60007 *Sir Nigel Gresley*, No. 71000 *Duke of Gloucester* and the 'Duchess' over three big hills, Grayrigg, Shap and Ais Gill. An out-of-sorts *Duchess of Hamilton* was beaten fair and square by *Duke of Gloucester*, but she was to come back from this setback and, in the last year of her boiler ticket, produce some of what Mike Notley thinks is the finest running that we have seen in preservation.

One of these later runs saw her back on her old stamping

ground and making, in terms of quality, one of the finest climbs of Shap, certainly in preservation and perhaps ever. This was on a charter organised by the now-defunct 'Days Out' operation, which organised special charter trains for enthusiasts. The train was 'The Caledonian' on 19 October 1996 when, with an 11-coach 435 tons gross load, she was checked to 44mph at the foot of the climb to Shap. Notley was on board:

She met the 1-in-75 at only 52½mph but Crewe driver Derek Lester and his fireman Bob Hart conjured up a gargantuan effort from the 4-6-2. Nowhere on the climb did they fall below 49mph and they passed the summit at 50½mph, an epic ascent that involved a maximum power output of close to 3,200hp. If you look at the list of fastest climbs of Shap, this run just makes it into the top twenty but in terms of quality it is arguably the best given the low speed she started the climb.

Her last runs were on 30 November and 31 December, when she hauled a 'Days Out' railtour from London to Glasgow, returning to York on the following day. She was the first Stanier 'Pacific' of any kind to climb Camden Bank since 1964, and an appropriate way for the locomotive now known by everyone simply as 'The Duchess' to bow out. The northbound journey was Les Jackson's last day driving on the railway, and his last steam turn, though his retirement was to prove short-lived as he would soon work for the nuclear flask train operator Direct Rail Services for a couple of years before hanging up his grease-top cap for the last time.

After a two-hour break at Crewe to refresh passengers and locomotive, Jackson took the regulator of No. 46229 on the route he'd been driving and firing for most of his professional life, and he made the most of it, arriving at Preston ninety seconds early, despite starting just over four minutes late. At Barton Loop, just under five miles north of Preston, the 'Duchess' refilled her tender with water, and took on 3,700 gallons, though Mike Notley reckoned it was hard to see how this had been used since Crewe. The twenty-eight-minute scheduled stop became a forty-eight-minute stop, but that didn't deter Les Jackson from trying to regain all the time he could.

Through Lancaster and Carnforth the 'Duchess' roared, gradually gaining time. It was the sign of a driver and fireman who knew their locomotive and the route intimately, but this superb performance had winded the locomotive, and with water in the boiler dropping, Jackson allowed speed to fall to 47mph at the summit as he girded the locomotive's loins for *Duchess of Hamilton*'s final climb of Shap to date. It wasn't the best climb ever, cresting the summit at 34.5mph. Just as the summit was passed, Jackson remembered his run of 1963 and closed the regulator. He'd had a premonition of a slip, and *Duchess of Hamilton* duly obliged, speed falling to 32mph before Jackson felt she was able to take much in the way of power without slipping further. Carlisle was reached on time, despite the delay. Jackson's skill and *Duchess of Hamilton*'s power were proved.

The following run the next day was a curious mixture of a funeral and a celebration of what the locomotive had achieved over the past sixteen years. The performances of

'The Duchess' had elevated her to the pantheon of loco-motive achievement, notably her efforts on Saunderton and the Settle–Carlisle. Many thousands of us hold fond memories of her during those years, and still miss her even now. *Duchess of Hamilton* would spend a couple of years visiting heritage railways, being tended with the gentle care she now needed. On some lines, it was possible, for a fee, to drive her, though on the Great Central it was felt that such was her power that only those who had already completed its driving courses would be able to do so.

Enthusiasts were soon to be given hope, however, as by now preparations were in place for her baton to be handed to another 'Duchess'.

Chapter Twenty-One
Baton Handed

Les Jackson's epic last run with *Duchess of Hamilton* marked a fitting climax to the locomotive's main-line career, but she only had a couple of years left before her mandatory ten-year boiler overhaul was due. It had already been decided that she would spend a period on static display at the National Railway Museum, but moves were already taking place that would ensure another 'Duchess' would soon be running. It wouldn't be the end – more the handing of the baton to another locomotive.

In 1989 Bressingham had bought *Duchess of Sutherland* from Butlin's and it wasn't long before thoughts started turning to getting her running again. After a four-week hire to the East Lancashire Railway, which runs between Bury and Ramsbottom, for static display at its Steam Railway Festival in August 1993 (which saw the locomotive temporarily disguised as No. 46246 *City of Manchester* in conjunction with the city's failed bid to host the 2000 Olympic Games) a study was made to see what work would be needed. An extensive list of work was produced, with overhaul estimated at around £162,000 – a tenfold increase on the cost incurred by Bressingham in the 1970s. The intention was that the ELR would pay Bressingham a hire fee to run the locomotive, but after looking at the figures, it was decided that the figures didn't add up commercially, and *Duchess of Sutherland* returned to Bressingham after what turned out to be a year-long sojourn in Lancashire.

In 1994, the Trustees of Bressingham asked the Princess Royal Class Locomotive Trust (PRCLT) if it would be interested in acquiring the 9½-inch gauge railway that ran around the gardens. The PRCLT had been formed to look after another ex-Butlin's engine, No. 46203 *Princess Margaret Rose*, which had been loaned to the Midland Railway Centre at Butterley, Derbyshire. The Trust had bought the locomotive and was running her on the main line very successfully, and it wasn't long before conversations started between its chairman, the construction businessman Brell Ewart, and David Ward, by now a Trustee of Bressingham, about *Duchess of Sutherland*.

Ewart is a no-nonsense businessman with a passion for steam and helped form the PRCLT. He speaks with a broad Derbyshire accent, and is direct, straightforward and down to earth. At this stage, Bressingham had no intention of selling No. 6233 but the dialogue was to prove highly useful. Things moved quickly, however, and in autumn 1995, while considering a bid by the Great Central Railway to host the locomotive on loan, the Trustees decided to sell *Duchess of Sutherland*. They immediately contacted Ewart, who recalls in *6233 Duchess of Sutherland and the Princess Coronation Class*:

> I received a telephone call from David Ward saying that the Trustees had decided, reluctantly, to sell *Duchess of Sutherland*. David said that they all wanted the PRCLT to

have 6233 in view of the facilities it had and also its track record with the earlier general overhaul and restoration of 46203 *Princess Margaret Rose* to main line running condition. What did I think?

I replied that I had not really ever thought about it but if that was what they thought than we had better say yes.

The Trustees were still considering the Great Central Railway's loan bid, and suddenly a bid was made by the Great Central for the locomotive of £200,000, which was more than the provisional figure of £175,000 agreed with Ewart. It presented the Trustees with a dilemma, as they had already offered the PRCLT first option on the locomotive, but they also had a duty to maximise the return of the locomotive to Bressingham. Their dilemma was solved when Ewart agreed to match the offer from the Great Central. They held a special meeting in November 1995 to discuss the sale of the locomotive, but in all truth, the reasons David Ward outlined for selecting the PRCLT still held true, though this wasn't to say that the Great Central wouldn't be able to look after the locomotive equally well.

There were factors at Bressingham, too, which made the sale of the locomotive a good move. Covered space was at a premium, and though *Duchess of Sutherland* was under cover, the fact was that she was too big to be displayed effectively. Furthermore, if restoration was ever to commence at Bressingham, the asbestos boiler lagging would have to be removed, and that would be a difficult, expensive and potentially dangerous task. What clinched it was that the locomotive had a buyer lined up willing to pay its market value — a value that it would never realise sitting at Bressingham. In turn, that money could be used on other exhibits there. Commercially it was a sound decision, but inevitably with such a dearly loved exhibit, there were mixed feelings about her departure.

Ewart went to Bressingham to agree the deal with Alan Bloom and have a look at *Duchess of Sutherland*.

After having a good look at 6233 and going inside the firebox, I went to the hall where Alan lives. We sat together at the kitchen table, had a cup of tea and agreed the deal, although Alan was very sad at letting 6233 go.

I feel that if it had been his decision alone it may not have been sold, but the board of Trustees had a duty to look after the long-term interests and well-being of the museum and 6233 couldn't generate cash to do that other than by its sale.

We shook hands on the deal, and I paid a 10% deposit. I left with very mixed emotions, feeling elated with the deal and the prospects that 6233 gave, but also very sad knowing that we were taking away a locomotive that Alan had given so much to since 1971. At the end of it all I reconciled this emotion by asking what was best for the locomotive. Clearly, a move to us, and with that the prospect of future running on the main line.

The sale was confirmed in November 1995, and was broadly welcomed by enthusiasts keen to see what had hitherto been regarded as something of a caged beast returned to working order on a line that gave her a chance to stretch her legs, though there were concerns that the return to steam of *Duchess of Sutherland* could mean a longer stay on display for *Duchess of Hamilton* than many predicted.

The cost of the purchase was beyond the PRCLT's limited resources, so Brell Ewart's company, Whitehouse Construction, footed the bill. Ewart was keen to expand into the railway civil engineering market, and, ever the canny businessman, he wanted to use *Duchess of Sutherland* to help promote this. A deal was agreed between Whitehouse Construction and the PRCLT that would see it eventually buy the locomotive from it once funds had been raised.

From then, things moved quickly, with movement by road from Bressingham to the PRCLT's base at Swanwick Junction, at the Midland Railway Centre, planned for 3 February 1996. (The tender had gone the day before.) Despite a couple of technical hitches with the road tractor unit, the locomotive was loaded safely onto the road trailer, and prepared to leave. While many at Bressingham arrived to pay their respects to one of the museum's flagship locomotives, it was too much for Alan Bloom, always a man who loved his locomotives, and he stayed indoors while *Duchess of Sutherland* departed for her new home. She arrived late that night, showered with flashes from photographers keen to mark her arrival. On 4 February she was gently unloaded and hauled by a diesel shunter into the PRCLT's West Shed, where she was reunited with her tender. She looked perfectly comfortable in her home, and she was stood next to her older cousin, *Princess Margaret Rose*. The picture was complete. The big challenge now was to fund her overhaul.

Chapter Twenty-Two
Reviving *Sutherland*

The PRCLT always planned to overhaul *Duchess of Sutherland* to main-line standards, but in 1997 its fundraising efforts were dealt a huge blow by the premature failure of its other 'Pacific', No. 46203 *Princess Margaret Rose*, with leaking tubes caused by the firebox walls thinning. The locomotive was being operated on main-line charter trains and revenue from these was intended to be used to restore the new arrival at Swanwick Junction. Now that revenue stream was over, there was growing pressure on the Trust to find alternatives, particularly because Whitehouse Construction wished (as it always had) to sell *Duchess of Sutherland* to it the following year.

The Trust considered all the options – borrowing money, appealing to the public, writing to well-known benefactors, but all were felt to stand little chance of success, and the Trust was probably right in this. A few years later, a public appeal for donations to buy No. 4472 *Flying Scotsman* would raise £350,000 in donations from the public, but that was for a much better-known locomotive than the largely unknown 'Duchess'.

At a meeting with the museums adviser from the East Midlands Museum Service, Lesley Colsell, she suggested making a bid for a Heritage Lottery Fund grant, and after considering its merits, the Trustees of the PRCLT agreed. The Heritage Lottery Fund was one of the more important things to come out of the National Lottery, and effectively provided a huge fund that heritage projects of all types could apply for. Railway preservationists had already had some successes in accessing this money, and the purchase and restoration of *Duchess of Sutherland* perfectly fitted the Fund's remit.

The application took months to complete, but in November 1997, after Brell Ewart and the Trust's vice-chairman, Chris Powell, had spent twelve hours at a photocopier, the documents were sent to the Heritage Lottery Fund's London headquarters, with fingers and toes firmly crossed. It can take a long time for the Fund to decide on the merits of a bid, and as the Trust's self-imposed deadline of 30 June 1998 to buy *Duchess of Sutherland* from Whitehouse Construction approached, nerves started to jangle: would the Trust's ambitious bid be successful – and even if it was, would it be announced in time? At this stage, Whitehouse Construction had to sell the locomotive, and if the PRCLT was unable to buy her, other bidders – including mysterious 'American businessmen' – could be given their chance.

With just four weeks to go, the Heritage Lottery Fund called the Trust asking for a meeting within two days, and for the locomotive to be valued by the Fund's man. Brell Ewart and Brian Radford showed Mr Goodheram from Cheffins auctioneers in Cambridge around the locomotive, and sat tight: things were starting to happen. Radford then took the initiative by telephoning the Heritage Lottery Fund to ask how the awards committee meeting had gone and got a positive reply, which he immediately passed on to Ewart. Then the Fund put it in writing: the PRCLT's ambitious bid was successful. The award was for a whopping £324,508, some 75% of the estimated purchase and overhaul cost of £432,677, and stipulated that the project must start in August.

Steam Railway described *Duchess of Sutherland* as 'the forgotten "Duchess"' when it reported the grant, and for many that had been the case for some time. No more – *Duchess of Sutherland* was back in the limelight.

At Swanwick Junction, meanwhile, preparations were well underway to start the restoration of *Duchess of Sutherland*, with the process laid down in simple terms in the application for Lottery funding. This essentially involved stripping the locomotive to her component parts, sending the boiler away to be repaired, and while that was being done, overhauling the chassis before finally refitting the boiler on the main frames and connecting everything up. The tender also needed an extensive overhaul before it could be attached to the locomotive.

Put like that, overhauling a steam locomotive sounds like a fairly straightforward exercise, but it's anything but. Fifty years ago, Crewe Works would have viewed getting the locomotive running as a straightforward exercise, and rather than repairing many parts, even including the boiler, it would simply replace them with spares. These days, of course, that's not an option for most of the locomotives as there simply aren't the spares out there. The restoration of *Duchess of Sutherland* would, by and large, be based around repairing any defective components (bar consumables such as boiler tubes, which are made out of easy-to-obtain material), and when you're dealing with a locomotive that hasn't been steamed for more than twenty years, and that was withdrawn forty-four years before, that's not a simple exercise. Brell Ewart headed the restoration team, with Brian Radford acting as consulting engineer, and the PRCLT's skilled maintenance staff performing much of the technical work. It was hoped the locomotive would return to steam in March 2000, which was regarded as a very tough timescale, but one that was felt to be achievable given that the Trust had restored *Princess Margaret Rose* in just sixteen months.

One of the key decisions that had to be made before significant work took place centred on the braking system. The 'Duchesses' were all built with vacuum brakes, which relied on a vacuum hose linking the locomotive and the carriages releasing the brakes. If the vacuum failed, either because the train had somehow separated, or because of a failure with the locomotive's equipment, the brakes would apply, making them failsafe, one of the railway's favourite terms. However, since the 1960s, new carriages had been built with compressed air brakes, which were quicker-acting and stronger. Though some sets of privately owned carriages were allowed to run on the main line with vacuum brakes, many more only had air brakes. The PRCLT had to decide whether to fit *Duchess of Sutherland* with air brakes in addition to her vacuum brakes, or to stick with what she had. The Trust looked at what future operating conditions would be and decided to spend the money installing air brakes during the overhaul, as retrofitting them would have been difficult and much more costly.

Though the workshops at Swanwick Junction were well equipped, some further equipment was needed, not least a set of lifting jacks so that the wheels of the 'Duchess' could be removed. A set of suitable jacks was made redundant by the new owner of Crewe Works, Adtranz (now Bombardier) and the PRCLT wasted no time in acquiring them. The stage was set. Some of the most crucial work had already been done shortly after *Duchess of Sutherland*'s arrival back in 1996. Her boiler was insulated with asbestos, and that had to be removed as soon as she arrived. (Actually, the work should have been done at Bressingham according to law, but an exemption was granted as the facilities at Swanwick were better.)

The overhaul took a major step forward in autumn 1998, when the boiler was lifted from the main frames. This is never a process for the faint-hearted, as a 'Duchess' boiler is a particularly heavy bit of kit. Before it could be removed, all the myriad fittings linking it with the chassis had to be carefully stripped off, and the locomotive moved outside for the lift to take place. A seventy-five-ton rail crane was used for the lift, and the boiler was placed on a low-loader for onward transport to the Severn Valley Railway's boiler shop at Bridgnorth, Shropshire. And this was where I first met *Duchess of Sutherland*, or at least, a very significant part of her. The Severn Valley Railway (SVR) is one of the few places left in Britain where the extensive and difficult repairs needed to locomotive boilers can be carried out, and there was no question that *Duchess of Sutherland*'s boiler needed a lot of work, particularly in the firebox.

Boilers are particularly vulnerable to wear and corrosion because of the temperatures and forces they have to deal with. In the firebox, a fire can be hot enough to melt the copper it's formed of, and this is only prevented by the heat transferring from the firebox into the water that surrounds it and fills the boiler. The boiler barrel, meanwhile, has to deal with similar temperatures, and with high-pressure steam. The inevitable expansion and contraction as steam is raised or dropped in the locomotive all place huge stresses on the metal. The only way anyone can tell exactly what a boiler's condition is is to separate it from the locomotive, and examine it in detail while it is cold and empty, and that's exactly what the SVR's boilersmiths did. The news wasn't good.

Parts of the firebox where pieces of copper were joined had burned away, and the outside wrapper plate had been gouged over years in service by caulking of one of the joints. Caulking involves hammering the metal to close any gaps, and if done too hard, or repeatedly over a long period, can cause this sort of damage. The tubeplate at the firebox end, which supports the tubes that carry the hot gases through the boiler, was very worn, and was even bulging in places. It meant that a new firebox tubeplate would be needed, and it would have to be made from scratch at Bridgnorth. Further investigations showed that the outer firebox was cracked too, something that could only be solved by cutting out the affected areas and welding in new copper. While the tubeplate at the front of the boiler was just about serviceable, there was no guarantee it would remain so for the ten years or so the locomotive was expected to steam, so it was decided to replace that too. The new tubeplates were made at Bridgnorth by hand over formers, solid patterns based on the original drawings. It was long, hard, hot work that left little margin for error. It is a mark of Bridgnorth's craftsmanship, and to the huge expansion in railway preservation's engineering capabilities, that this was able to take place at all.

Some of the repairs needed the boiler to be turned onto its side, and it was this sight that greeted me in 1999 when I attended a volunteer induction day at the Severn Valley Railway. Prospective volunteers for the line were given a tour of all the departments so they could choose which area they wanted to work in. I'd always fancied working on steam locomotives, but the sight of *Duchess of Sutherland*'s boiler on its side in the workshop floored me. I knew the 'Duchesses' were big, of course, but with the boiler on its side, you could see the whole of the underside of the firebox, and it must have been as big as – perhaps bigger than – the box room at my parents' house.

Gradually the SVR's boilersmiths got to grips with their demanding tasks, and eventually it came together as its designer intended. According to Brian Radford and Brell Ewart, it needed 600 replacement rivets, more than 500 stays (which are screw-like components that keep the inner and outer fireboxes separate), forty linear feet of copper welding, and, of course, the two new tubeplates. It was one of the most comprehensive boiler repairs at the time, and certainly the most thorough 'Duchess' repair since Crewe Works outshopped its last 'Duchesses' in the 1960s.

At Swanwick, while the boiler was being worked on at Bridgnorth, the PRCLT's team got to grips with stripping the rest of the engine and overhauling it. With the boiler off the main frames, shot-blasting was the best option for stripping the paint and corrosion, and railway preservation was much more experienced at it than when Bressingham tried it in the 1970s. The six big driving wheels were removed and sent to the Severn Valley for tyre reprofiling, leaving the front bogie and rear truck to support the frames. On inspection, the frames turned out to be in good condition, with just a few broken rivets and fractures in areas that were easily replaceable. Brell Ewart, ever keen to lead by example, took on the majority of the shot-blasting, and as each section was cleaned and then painted, the years rolled off *Duchess of Sutherland*.

The frames were painted black on the outside faces, and red on the inside, a long-standing railway tradition, and with easy access, the complicated pipework for lubrication systems was installed and repaired. This was easier said than done as the pipes had to be installed perfectly to prevent other components rubbing against them and breaking them. The workshop floor was covered in sundry parts of *Duchess of Sutherland* being worked on in a close preservation equivalent to the great railway works that built steam locomotives, and bit by bit, as the likes of driving wheels returned, the jigsaw puzzle of rebuilding the locomotive took shape.

In early 2000, the boiler was finally completed and returned to Swanwick Junction on 25 March. A new smoke-box was needed, something that had been known about from the start, and this was being made as the boiler arrived.

Before its installation, it was decided to trial-fit the boiler onto the chassis, which was now virtually complete. This made sense as some new fittings – notably connected with the new air brakes – had been installed, and a test-fit would highlight any parts that needed to be moved. To try to do that with the boiler on is a task that can only be imagined, but it wouldn't have been easy or pleasant. Some of the air brake pipes were found to foul the doors on the ashpan, but thanks to the test-fitting of the boiler, once it was removed, it was a fairly straightforward task to re-route them.

Before the boiler could be permanently reunited with *Duchess of Sutherland*'s chassis, the steam test had to be performed. This is perhaps the most crucial of all checks on a steam locomotive as the consequences of a major fault in the boiler don't bear thinking about. Before any fire is allowed to be lit, all steam locomotive boilers are subjected to a hydraulic test to a level significantly above the operating pressure. The normal operating pressure of *Duchess of Sutherland* was 250psi, so the hydraulic test would subject the boiler to a whopping 375psi. Using water means that any leaks are easily spotted, and if the boiler passes the hydraulic test, then it should work perfectly with steam at its normal operating pressure.

So it proved, and *Duchess of Sutherland*'s boiler passed its hydraulic test on 22 June 2000. The stage was set for the first fire to be lit in her firebox since 1976. The first time you light a fire in a boiler, you have to take things gently, building up steam pressure gradually so as not to stress everything too much: things could still go wrong, and this minimises the risks as any faults should become apparent very quickly when pressure is low. There were no problems with *Duchess of Sutherland*, and, after three days of gentle warming, the safety valves lifted on 30 June 2000: *Duchess of Sutherland* was now officially alive.

The boiler was allowed to cool for three days before being flushed out to remove the inevitable bits of scale and other debris that sit inside, and the team set to work on completing the cosmetic cladding on the outside of the boiler. Over the next month this (and the insulation that it covers) was fitted everywhere except on the craning points, and the boiler was reunited with the frames on 28 July 2000 – it wouldn't be long now before *Duchess of Sutherland* turned her wheels in anger.

Getting the boiler back on the frames was undoubtedly a big landmark but there was much still to do. All the control gear and gauges had to be fitted, and this is often a fiddly process. One thing that few noticed about the locomotive now that she was nearing completion was that she was actually two inches lower than when built. The company that owned the main-line network, Railtrack, stipulated that the maximum height allowed for all rolling stock was 13ft 1 inch, in order to ensure that trains didn't touch overhead electric wires, or the many low bridges and tunnels that dot our largely Victorian network. The PRCLT had already lowered *Princess Margaret Rose* by reducing the height of some boiler fittings such as the dome and chimney, and the cab, and had done the same to *Duchess of Sutherland*. It made no difference to the locomotive in performance terms, and so well was it done that only an expert would notice the difference. It meant that when the time came, the routes

Duchess of Sutherland could operate on would be far wider-ranging than if the alterations hadn't taken place.

All this work takes time, and the inevitable result was that the group's planned steaming date of March 2000 had been missed, but this sort of project is always open to fate, and no short cuts can be taken to speed things up. By January 2001, *Duchess of Sutherland* was complete and ready to make her first moves since 1976. The atmosphere at Swanwick was electric as the fire was gradually built up on 17 January, and the eagle-eyes, ears and noses of the restoration team were constantly twitching, alert to the first sign of anything amiss. The following day, pressure had built up nicely, and at 1338, the regulator was inched open. Steam flowed from the main steam pipe in the boiler, through the barely open regulator valve, and into the cylinders. After a few seconds came the moment thousands had been waiting for for twenty-five years, as the steam pressure built up in the cylinders and started to move the pistons: *Duchess of Sutherland* had finally moved under her own power for the first time since 1976.

The 'forgotten Duchess' would be thrust into the limelight. The celebrations were for later. Before then, as many of the powered systems as possible had to be tested before the locomotive could venture more than a few yards. As the tests were passed, clearance was given for her to venture onto the Midland Railway Centre's running line. Gently at first, she was steamed to Pye Bridge, stretching her steel limbs gradually as if she'd been asleep for the previous quarter-century. As the lubrication bedded in, she was allowed to run along the whole length of the line to Buttcrley and then back.

As always a few minor glitches showed themselves on the first run, but these were soon put right and the locomotive granted approval to start a lengthy running-in period that demanded she cover 1,000 miles without significant trouble. This running-in period is mandatory for all steam locomotives that are to operate on the main line, and with good reason. The privatised railway has strict targets for train punctuality and liability, and if an operator's train fails and causes someone else's to run late, there can be financial penalties. Steam locomotives are allowed to work on the main line only after meeting the highest reasonable standards for their overhaul and operation. They have to share the tracks with 125mph passenger trains and heavy freights, fast-accelerating local services and all-stations stoppers, and that means they have to be reliable. Given that the youngest steam locomotive that could possibly operate on the main line is forty-eight years old (No. 92220 *Evening Star*), these old machines can be frail and temperamental, and to minimise the risks of them failing with a charter train and delaying other timetabled trains, an extensive running-in programme is required. (At the time of writing, the assertion that the youngest steam locomotive that could be used on the main line is forty-eight years old – though it's unlikely that that locomotive will ever be restored – is correct. However, by the time of publication, the first new main-line steam locomotive to be built in Britain since 1960, No. 60163 *Tornado*, should be hauling passengers.)

While running-in was taking place, *Duchess of Sutherland* was receiving the final touch, the glorious coat of LMS 'Midland Red' that was used on the first unstreamlined

'Duchesses' in 1938. Bob Timmins of Cleobury Mortimer, Shropshire, undertook the work, and did a fabulous job, with *Duchess of Sutherland* appearing with her LMS number of 6233. It was now time for the PRCLT to jump through the final few hoops before *Duchess of Sutherland* could operate on the main line.

Throughout the restoration programme, a close liaison was maintained with Railtrack to ensure the locomotive would meet its demanding requirements. So smooth and well managed was the process that approval was quickly granted for first a run on the main line with two coaches of the PRCLT for 4 July, and for a loaded test run with a full train on 18 July. The purposes of these runs were twofold: first to ensure the locomotive ran properly, and that all safety systems worked, and secondly to test the brakes under full load and emergency conditions. As 4 July dawned, the years of hard work and dedication – and money – would be put to the test.

Gingerly *Duchess of Sutherland* left the sanctuary of the Midland Railway Centre and waited at the signal that would give her access to the main line. The route planned was a circular one to Derby, then on to Chesterfield, Beighton, Sheffield, and back to Swanwick, twice. *Duchess of Sutherland* was kept at the signal for more than an hour before easing onto the main line, and then reversing so she was on the correct track. A points failure at the junction meant that a track gang had to be called, and after further delay, No. 6233 finally headed towards Derby, already two hours late. The move caught the normally thoroughly informed railway photography community by surprise, and only a few got out to witness this historic run, but those who did will long remember it. After thirty-seven years, *Duchess of Sutherland* was on the main line and running well.

Railtrack thought so too, and granted approval for the loaded test run to take place. This time it was a much more suitable load for a 'Duchess' of fourteen carriages, with each of the 670 seats taken for *Duchess of Sutherland*'s first revenue-earning train since 1964. July 18 was a cloudy affair not best suited to railway photography, but that didn't stop enthusiasts from all over Britain crowding stations on the route to pay homage to a returning icon. It's a cliché to say that people flocked to the lineside, but that's exactly what happened – five long years after *Duchess of Hamilton* left the main-line scene, a 'Duchess' was back in business.

In a perfect world, *Duchess of Sutherland* would have run faultlessly and returned to the Midland Railway Centre in a blaze of glory, but it is an imperfect world we live in, and one of those faults you simply can't predict struck near Dronfield station when the braking system failed and automatically applied itself. The air pressure in the braking system had gone, and with no obvious repair possible, a diesel was summoned to haul the train via Chesterfield to Derby, from where another pair of diesels hauled *Duchess of Sutherland* back to Swanwick. It was an inglorious end to what should have been a glorious debut, but the fault had to be rectified before the locomotive could be given a clean bill of health. It was traced to a valve on the locomotive's air compressor being too tight, and after the green light had been given to make an adjustment by Railtrack, final approval for *Duchess of Sutherland* to operate on charter trains was granted. After all the efforts to ensure her reliability, the failure was a bitter blow for the team to take – but one that made all the staff and volunteers of the PRCLT more determined than ever not to let happen again.

Chapter Twenty-Three
Power Behind the Throne

Duchess of Sutherland was back on the main line, but getting a locomotive to that stage is one thing; it is quite another keeping it maintained and serviced to the standards required. Money is always a consideration, but the people who keep steam locomotives running are every bit as important. The railway preservation movement depends very largely on volunteer input – taken as whole, it must be one of the most remarkable volunteer-based operations in Britain, and the Princess Royal Class Locomotive Trust is no exception.

One of the main benefits claimed for the Modernisation Plan of 1955 was the reduction in labour that the new diesels and electrics would bring, and it's one of the few points of that flawed plan that brooks no argument, for steam locomotives are quite unbelievably labour-intensive machines. It's rather like looking after a horse – a steam locomotive has to be prepared before it can run, watched over while it's running, and swept out once it's arrived back on its home shed, and none of those tasks is simple.

We've seen through a number of eyewitness accounts how dirty and demanding driving and firing a steam locomotive is, and nothing has changed. A locomotive as big as Duchess of Sutherland demands a band of followers willing to help look after her, often at unsociable hours doing hard work that they wouldn't consider as a paid job, and all for nothing. I know, because while I was at university, I volunteered as an engine cleaner at the Severn Valley Railway's Bewdley shed. Yet such is the attraction of the iron horse that there are willing hands all around the country who dedicate as much time as they can to keeping steam alive, and one of the things I was keen to do when I was planning the book was to talk to some of the people who dedicate themselves to keeping a 'Duchess' running.

The first thing that strikes you at PRCLT's depot at the Midland Railway at Butterley, near Swanwick in Derbyshire, is how clean it is. Having written in an earlier chapter about the wonderful atmosphere in engine sheds, the PRCLT's base, the West Shed, might come as something of a shock if you're expecting coal dust and smoke, because there's hardly any of the stuff to be seen. It is amongst, if not the, most modern steam depot in Britain, and is far more like a modern diesel depot than any steam shed I've ever been to. There are no oil stains on the concrete floor, or piles of ash and clinker waiting to be disposed of; it's light and airy, calm, ordered and professional, the exact image that the Trust wants to project. It's also much better for visitors, because nobody likes getting smart clothes dirty on a day out. In a very real sense, it is twenty-first century railway preservation.

The shed was built in 1996 to house the PRCLT's collection of locomotives, and it's been extended since to house a museum, library and other facilities aimed at improving the interpretation of the Trust's exhibits. The site is split into two halves. The rear half is used for restoration of the Trust's non-steaming locomotives, and one of its tank engines is being overhauled by volunteers and full-time staff. The front is used to house the other locomotives when they're at Swanwick, as well as the museum. On the day I visited, *Duchess of Sutherland* was at Crewe being prepared for a main-line tour at the weekend, so the only locomotive there was the Trust's other 'Pacific' No. 46203 *Princess Margaret Rose* – and the two narrow-gauge diesel-powered locomotives that look very much like 'Princess Royals'.

The PRCLT's curator, Kate Smith, is a young lady in her twenties, and she's in charge of the museum. A trained curator with an interest in heritage in general rather than railways in particular, she's enthusiastic about the Trust, and is bright and bubbly – she's far removed from the austere curators of museums in the past. There's no question that Kate and the PRCLT have done a great job with the museum and interpretation of the locomotives and other exhibits, which include some former Royal Train coaches, and the LMS dynamometer car used on *Coronation*'s 114mph run in the 1930s. There's a small cinema where one can choose to watch a selection of railway documentaries, a room that tells the story of the Trust's locomotives, but most fascinating of all is a replica of William Stanier's office, complete with a moving mannequin of Sir William himself. It's not the biggest museum in the world, but it is very good and well worth a visit (as is the wider Midland Railway complex at Butterley) when trains are operating.

And the engineering facilities are impressive too. It's not Crewe Works, for sure, but the facilities are good enough to undertake the lion's share of restoration work on a

'Duchess', and include some very sophisticated kit. Perhaps the most impressive bit is the locomotive weighing equipment, which is fitted in one of the inspection pits. For any repairs to the locomotive other than routine servicing, it's vital that the locomotive weighs what it should, and more importantly that the weight is distributed correctly. Even changing a spring could, if it was done incorrectly, alter the weight distribution of a locomotive, and that's bad news for everyone. If a locomotive was allowed to run in such a state, it could damage the track, and it could damage itself. That's why the weight has to be verified after every significant running repair, and the PRCLT's weighing equipment is modern and easy to use, making this crucial task a little easier than before.

The library is a really smart room, with plenty of space for work – and that was where I met some of the volunteers. Things were looking promising, and so they proved when a handful of volunteers came in for a chat over a cup of tea. Because I visited on a Wednesday, all were retired, but there are plenty of younger volunteers with full-time jobs who come at weekends. It's certainly not true to say that railway preservation is the preserve of any particular age group.

Or indeed gender, because one of the volunteers I met was Trish Birks, a lady who had only been volunteering for a few weeks. Trish called herself a trainee volunteer, but I suspect she's probably rather more clued-up than she lets on. She works at the West Shed, but she also helps on the PMR railtours in the sales department. Her view on why she does it is simple: 'This is a wonderful thing, and it needs all the help it can get.' Although railway preservation is male-dominated, it's a remarkably open movement, and Trish certainly didn't seem overawed or bothered by her male counterparts.

'My partner was very interested in steam, and we simply got more and more interested and decided to volunteer,' she told me. They'd been regular passengers on charter trains organised by the PRCLT's charter arm, PMR tours, and like so many volunteers, Trish felt that she wanted to put something back into the organisation. She's a cheery lady, waving off the odd bit of banter and giving the men as good as they give.

And banter (almost all unprintable, sadly) was something that underpinned the meeting – there was a lot of chat of railways in general, and of steam in particular, mostly quite technical stuff about the niceties of fitting boiler tubes and so on, but always with a smile. It may be hard work, but it's fun work too.

One of the more experienced volunteers is John Riley, an engineer by trade who's been involved in the PRCLT for many years. John's a typical engineer in that he's very understated (when he met the Queen on the Royal Train, he described the experience as 'very nice') but the passion comes through. Oddly for an engineer, he's very talkative, and Trish and the others invariably have to interrupt him when they want to say something, but it's all done with good humour. One of the things John likes best is the feel of having to prove oneself on the main line. 'It's the challenge – you get a locomotive and prove to the authorities that volunteers can restore a locomotive to main-line standards. It's good for amateurs like us to prove that we can do as good a job as the professionals – even though we probably have to be even better than the pros to pass muster.'

It's this determination to succeed that's at the heart of the preservation movement, and John is backed by a more recent arrival, Michael Hockaday. Michael looks like a fit fifty-year-old, but in reality, he's rather older than that. His background was in an office, and he has something of the look of an architect about him: he's educated and well-spoken, and working at the West Shed is quite a contrast with his professional career. He's also one of the few people who can keep John Riley from bubbling away for a few minutes.

'I'd had a few trips as a passenger and decided to become a patron, and then I decided to put my body where my money was,' he says. Hockaday helped paint the extension to the West Shed, and enjoyed getting his hands dirty: 'I worked in an office, and I never thought I'd get involved with a steam engine. It takes four people to remove a boiler tube – I've learned skills I thought I'd never gain.'

And he thoroughly enjoys helping *Duchess of Sutherland*: 'I like meeting people and getting to know our passengers – you see familiar faces quite often, and you build up a rapport. I see a lot of families, and you know, some of the kids seem to know as much about the train as we do!'

He's one of the volunteer stewards on the PMR charter trains when he's not at Swanwick working in the shed, and he's one of more than ten in each train – one per coach – tasked with keeping passengers happy. It's a non-stop job, keeping passengers informed, talking to them about the PRCLT (though never with a hard sell) and sharing their passion for the locomotive, for steam, and for railways in general. It really does make such a difference to a railtour, and Hockaday and his colleagues must be doing a good job as other charter train companies have asked the PRCLT to provide stewards for their trains!

Of course, it's not always plain sailing, and when things go wrong, as they do from time to time, a completely different set of skills is required, keeping passengers in the loop, and ensuring they'll be able to get home. On one occasion, everything was set for a tour to run, and the stewards were on the platforms with passengers patiently waiting for the train to come. Time ticked by with no sign of it. A track problem further up the line had prevented the train from leaving the depot, and it had to be cancelled. Dealing with disappointed passengers who may have travelled a long way for the tour is something few people would do for money, so for volunteers to do it for nowt is genuinely remarkable. They also have to keep the carriages clean inside, and inform everyone about any faults. 'If there are faults, it's the stewards that cop it!' says Hockaday.

The volunteers perform a huge number of roles supporting the PRCLT. One of the most crucial is acting as stewards on the charter trains the society promotes under the PMR Tours banner. These tours are the main revenue stream for the Trust, and ensuring passengers are happy is absolutely critical: the old maxim that if you upset a customer they'll tell ten of their friends, while if you do a really good job they'll only tell three is as true for running charter trains with *Duchess of Sutherland* as it is with anything else.

For Phil Ecclestone, another man in his fifties, it's his father's fault. 'My Dad was a driver on the West Coast Main Line and drove "Duchesses". You grow up with it – it gets into your blood. I started as a paying passenger, but I was made to feel so welcome and got to know the PRCLT people, so I became a patron and then a volunteer. Over the years, I've worked my way through – I've done a bit of everything in the workshop.'

The social side is important too, as John Sconlon explains: 'I've always been a steam enthusiast, and I've been here three years now. I don't have any particular skills, but I help out where I can, and I've made a lot of good friends.'

This is something universal in railway preservation in my experience. You can't put a bunch of people with a shared passion together and not make new friends, and though the growing professionalism of heritage railways means the nights of a session in the pub and turning up on duty the next morning are long gone (and very much *verboten* by the authorities too), an awful lot of volunteers spend all day working at a railway and then socialise outside the railway with their colleagues. Many hobbies have that sense of shared purpose, and railway preservation is no exception: the social side is very important, and many people have made lots of new friends by volunteering at heritage railways and societies. Some have done more than that, though: the National Railway Museum's Head of Knowledge and Collections, Helen Ashby, met her husband while they were working in *Duchess of Hamilton*'s support crew in the 1980s – who says the romance of the railways is dead?

The desire to learn new (or should that be old?) skills –

willingly passed on by paid staff – and more is fundamental to many people's experience of railway preservation. The trains *Duchess of Sutherland* works can start from all over the country, and that can mean some very long travel for the crews just to get to the starting point. Most of the volunteers are based within an hour or so of Swanwick Junction, but when the tours start from outside the Midlands, the distances start to mount up. And when you consider that preparation usually starts long before the train runs, the dedication of the volunteers is amplified.

If a tour runs on a Saturday, as many of them do, and the tour starts from near Swanwick, things are simplified, but the work starts on the Wednesday before, if not earlier. Preparing *Duchess of Sutherland* takes time, particularly if she hasn't worked for a couple of weeks and the boiler is cold. The fire is started a couple of days before the tour, and the locomotive is gently brought round from her slumber. While this is being done, checks are made on all the safety-critical systems that can be inspected before the boiler pressure has risen – and they will be double-checked closer to departure too.

The day before the tour, more volunteers will arrive to clean *Duchess of Sutherland*, though it's entirely possible this process will have been started before then, depending on numbers. Cleaning a steam locomotive is very different from washing your car, and not just because of its size. The various projections and access hatches and panels mean that putting it through a carriage washer isn't an option – doing so could damage the locomotive and the washer, so it has to be done the old-fashioned way using manual labour. The process is started by going over the locomotive with dry rags to remove any loose dirt from the surfaces, but this is only the first step. With as much of the dust and grime as possible removed, the volunteers then set to work with the time-honoured mixture of lubricating oil and paraffin. It sounds an odd mixture but it works very well, dissolving the oil stains and sooty marks that are an inevitable feature of steam operation, and applying a sheen to the paint. This has to be polished pretty quickly as a sticky oily residue on the paint-work is the last thing anyone wants. It takes an age to do, and some railways use wax polish instead, but the PRCLT maintains that the old way is the best.

Cleaning the paintwork is one thing, and you get a real sense of satisfaction from seeing your face reflected in it as you clean it, but attention is also paid to the connecting and coupling rods, and all the other external parts of the valve gear. These can pick up an awful amount of dirt, and if the motion is dirty, as one of the most visible parts, it quickly attracts attention, so the lubricating oil and paraffin is used here too. Done well – and the 'Duchess' is invariably done *very* well – the solution leaves a sheen on the rods that reflects the light, making them appear almost as if they are made of stainless steel.

Preparation of the locomotive continues, with the smoke-box being emptied of chars as during lighting up they will still be carried through the boiler tubes, and all drivers want a clear smokebox before they start work on the charter. As the day progresses and pressure builds ever closer to the maximum, more checks are made, and the sandboxes and lubricators filled. The driver and fireman on the day will check them too, but if these are ready for the off, no time will be wasted in filling them.

The likelihood is that the carriages will come from the train operator West Coast Railways, which operates the trains for the PRCLT, and these will be prepared thoroughly before the journey. Volunteers will make sure the carriages are clean, and if possible that apparatus such as lighting and heating systems work. Only when all are satisfied are they cleared for the train. On the day, the locomotive and carriages will be ready some hours in advance, usually meaning another early start for the support crew, and then, if everything goes to plan, the train will pick up its passengers and go to its destination.

On arrival, the support crew will help coal and water the locomotive, and the stewards clean the carriages for the return journey. They will then accompany the train to its starting point, ensure all the passengers have left safely, and clean the carriages once more. For those directly involved with *Duchess of Sutherland* there is still work to do. If she returns to Swanwick Junction, the first task will be to clean the firebox and smokebox, and ensure the tender and boiler are full of water. Then, if the locomotive isn't required for a while, volunteers will have to gently run the fire down so she can cool off gently. This can take anything up to three or four days, meaning that at some point every day for a week, *Duchess of Sutherland* will require care and attention. That's dedication.

We mustn't forget that organisations like the PRCLT have to make money to cover the costs of operating the locomotives, of paid staff, of bills and the like, and then try to keep some of what's left in hand for the next overhaul. And things aren't cheap. Using *Duchess of Sutherland* on the PRCLT's own tours means not paying between £6,000 and £10,000 a time to hire a locomotive, but they still have to pay West Coast Railways, the company that supplies the driver, fireman, guard and coaches, for its services – and, while West Coast Railways never divulges any information of this sort, drivers on scheduled services for the rail franchises earn something like £35,000 a year. Add to that the price of coal, which can be up to £200 a ton (and we know how much coal the 'Duchesses' burn), and you have a seriously expensive operation.

The 229 Club, the organisation that supports *Duchess of Hamilton*, and which was established in the 1990s, has had a slightly different focus in recent years, as their locomotive hasn't been operational since the 1990s, and is not expected to be overhauled for a good while, so it's tried to continue fundraising. Its chairman is chartered civil engineer, certified project manager and lifelong railwayman Donald Heath, a man now in his late sixties. He became involved in the 229 Club in the late 1990s when the outgoing chairman (and fellow career railwayman) Frank Patterson asked him to help. Heath has worked all over Britain, and his signal achievement was probably managing the electrification programme on the East Coast Main Line, from London to Edinburgh, between 1984 and 1991.

Heath is quite different from the rose-tinted enthusiast you might imagine. Years on the railway have imbued him with a healthy pragmatism, but he's very clear about what it is he appreciates about the 'Duchesses'. 'I drove it on the

East Lancashire Railway in the 1990s, and I've never felt such unbridled power,' he says. 'I've driven diesel, electric and other steam locomotives, but nothing compares.'

Supporters of the 229 Club pay a minimum of £10 a month to support the locomotive, with the aim of raising funds for its overhaul, and when *Duchess of Hamilton* was running on the main line, many of them got involved in the support crews. Since her withdrawal, though, numbers of supporters have declined. But Heath remains optimistic: the current re-streamlining of the locomotive is expected to generate a huge amount of interest, and even though an eventual overhaul to working order could cost the best part of a million pounds, 'I don't think we'll have much problem raising funds,' he says. It's testimony to the appeal of the 'Duchess' that even with *Flying Scotsman* part of the National Railway Museum's stable, a working *Duchess of Hamilton* may well approach even the draw of that locomotive.

What surprised even me was how few volunteers organisations like the PRCLT have, considering the demands placed on them. Every train operated by PMR tours requires around twenty volunteers to see it through, and the Trust only has around sixty volunteers in total – all able to give varying amounts of time – to keep *Duchess of Sutherland* in the pampered luxury to which she's accustomed. They give their labour for free, and most incur costs in travelling to and from the West Shed or wherever they're needed for main-line tours.

I left the West Shed impressed with the PRCLT's facilities, and, more importantly, by the dedication of the volunteers who help keep it running. Their passion and drive augers well for the future, and there are a good few youngsters involved as well. It's a hard, often physical, thing to do, but the sense of satisfaction one gets seeing a steam locomotive you've worked on running is worth all the effort.

The volunteers of the PRCLT, however, have an extraordinary story under their belt that shows just how highly regarded railway preservation is, because their locomotive played a part in the Queen's Golden Jubilee celebrations that takes my breath away even now.

Chapter Twenty-Four
Railway Royalty

The Royal Train is, depending on your point of view, either a glorious national institution or a huge waste of money: a spectacle to be savoured or one to be scrapped. The critics argue that members of the Royal Family can be transported quicker and more cheaply by air. The costs of the train, they say, outweigh the benefits. On the other hand, the train can save money too. If ever a member of the Royal Family has to stay overnight on a visit, a huge security operation springs into action, with areas sealed off, manhole covers welded, and so on. These costs are often borne in part by the local police force. By comparison, the Royal Train is already secure, and can be stabled at a suitable location easily and without the costs of the security operation involved during an overnight stay elsewhere.

At the start of the century, the arguments seemed very much weighted against retaining the train, and it looked like its 'last hurrah' would be during the Queen's Golden Jubilee year, 2002. Against the odds, however, an event that even five years before would have been laughed out of court was to contribute very strongly to a change of heart – and it required *Duchess of Sutherland* to make it happen. The plan was for *Duchess of Sutherland* to be the first standard gauge steam locomotive to haul the Royal Train carrying the reigning monarch since 1967. (*Flying Scotsman* had carried the Queen Mother in the 1980s when it hauled the train to open North Woolwich Railway Museum).

It was the editor of *RAIL*, Nigel Harris, who got the ball rolling. He had previously edited its sister magazine *Steam Railway* and he was (and is) an expert on our railways past and present. Much of the time he's a laconic Lancastrian bloke with a ready sense of humour – one of life's born raconteurs, if you will – but at others, particularly as the magazines went to press, he was always in the thick of the action, and had a scary eye for detail. Harris knew the Royal Train Foreman, Chris Hillyard, well. Hillyard is one of the railway's true gentlemen. He had worked at Wolverton since 1973, and had worked on the Royal Train for twenty-four years. He's a dignified man with a soft Northampton-shire burr, and is amongst the most respected men on the railway. Harris had been talking to Hillyard about how the Royal Train operated and what the true financial picture of it was, as there had been a lot of coverage in the media of its alleged high costs and lack of use. As ever, Harris wanted the complete picture from the people who knew best.

After talking through the train's finances, they sat in a small room at Wolverton that houses an extensive collection of relics connected with the Royal Train and had a coffee. As Harris was stirring a sugar into his drink, he casually asked Hillyard: 'I don't think you've ever had a steam locomotive on these carriages, have you?'

'No, we haven't,' replied Hillyard.

'Do you fancy it?'

'Yes I do, but there's all sorts of considerations – I don't think it would ever happen.'

At this point most people would expect the conversation to move on, but Harris's brain was whirring round at lightspeed, trying to think of a locomotive group with a suitable locomotive that might be able to keep the possibility of a steam-hauled Royal Train secret. Quick as a flash, he offered to put Hillyard in touch with Brell Ewart, the chairman of the PRCLT. Harris knew Ewart was one of the most resolutely professional men in preservation, and that he could keep a secret. Hillyard said he'd look at the idea but that it wasn't likely it would come to fruition. After agreeing to help Hillyard and Ewart make contact, Harris called the PRCLT's chairman. 'Would the 6233 team be interested in hauling the Royal Train?' he asked. Ewart didn't need asking twice. 'Yes, absolutely,' he replied.

Ewart quickly wrote to Matthew Golton, the general manager of the Rail Express Systems division of the freight company EWS. Rail Express Systems operated mail trains all over Britain, and provided the locomotives and drivers for the Royal Train, as well as many steam-hauled charters. Soon Golton and Ewart were discussing the fine detail of its operation, should approval be granted by the Royal Household and Her Majesty. Golton warned that even if approval was forthcoming, it would not be easy to make it happen. Approval did come quickly, the Palace enthusiastic about the concept, providing the operational and technical issues could be ironed out.

A small group of PRCLT Trustees was assembled to handle this secret operation. Brell Ewart, as chairman, was naturally involved, as was David Ward, who had been responsible for the Royal Train during his time with

InterCity, BR's long-distance passenger operation. Brian Radford was chosen for his engineering expertise (he had helped design the Royal Train coaches), and Howard Routledge was a former police sergeant who had worked on several royal visits. It was made clear from the start that secrecy was paramount.

EWS was looking at the itinerary for the Royal Train and identified a day when the Queen would be visiting North Wales as suitable, and forwarded the request to the Royal Household, which gave its blessing in a matter of days. This meant that *Duchess of Sutherland*'s planned outings on the North Wales Coast line between Chester and Holyhead on 14 and 21 October 2001 presented a perfect opportunity for a rehearsal. The first run was chosen, and staff from Railtrack, First North Western (the local passenger train operator on the line), the British Transport Police, EWS, the police and the Royal Train staff were picked. The crew of the train was formed of staff who would be involved on the day. It was as close as possible to being a dress rehearsal, and anyone who asked about their presence – whether PRCLT volunteers or curious passengers – was told that Railtrack was auditing the operation, though thankfully nobody had to explain how or why.

Particular attention was paid to the proposed overnight stabling site for the train at Valley, Anglesey. Nuclear flask trains regularly visited the Nuclear Electric plant there, and there was a turning triangle that would be vital for ensuring *Duchess of Sutherland* was facing the right way. The route, date and times were now all decided. *Duchess of Sutherland* would haul the Royal Train from Valley to Crewe on 11 June

2002, stopping en route to pick up and drop off the royal party. Further checks on the locomotive and support coach were made to ensure that the air brake pipes were compatible with those on the Royal Train (they should have been and were but these sorts of details always seem to bite back if they're not checked). Increasingly, the PRCLT found itself hosting visitors from EWS, Railtrack and other organisations checking details out about No. 6233 and the PRCLT's operations. In view of the need for secrecy, those outside the handful who knew were told that they were being scrutinised for possible repeat work on the main line. Though it was never said, the implication was that a regular deal to haul a luxury train was on the cards.

As the PRCLT went into 2002, *Duchess of Sutherland*'s main-line schedule was worked around the Royal Train operation, as a fair length of time before the date would be needed for final preparations and security checks. As the new year gathered pace, Brell Ewart started researching how the locomotive should be presented, and found photographs of a special headboard the London Midland Region used on all of its named trains during Coronation week in 1953. He asked EWS if a replica could be carried, and after consulting with the Royal Household, permission was granted for this embellishment.

With spring well underway, it was becoming increasingly clear that at least some information would have to be given to volunteers who would be involved on the day about what was planned. After much discussion, the go-ahead was given for a limited and strictly embargoed release of information to certain volunteers. At a meeting of Trustees in April, Ewart kept his powder dry, despite being allowed to share his news. When the subject moved on to other business, he spoke up. 'I've got some of my own,' he said, and revealed what had been going on for the previous few months. The reaction was stunned silence. So effective had the efforts at secrecy been that nobody had any idea. Gradually the news sank in and discussions started about who should form the support crew. Just as it had been in steam days, people were selected on the basis of seniority and experience. The game was on.

The headboard was by now being finalised, and Brian Radford had discovered that the London Midland Region had kept a special set of four headlamps for the Royal Train at Camden. The lamp manufacturer John Beesley was commissioned to make five lamps – four for the engine and one for presentation to the Queen – in two batches of two, and later, one, hopefully ensuring that nobody would put two and two together and make four! Said Beesley, 'I was given to believe I was making two pairs of lamps – one pair for *Duchess of Sutherland* and another for *Princess Margaret Rose*, but my instructions were to supply the lamps in undercoat rather than the usual white finish, which made me suspicious.'

The final order for the single presentation lamp confirmed it: the order included the comment 'You may have guessed what the lamps were for'. From then on, they were referred to as the 'Grove Train headlamps', as 'Grove' was the codeword used by the LMS for the Royal Train.

As the number of people who knew about *Duchess of Sutherland* hauling the Royal Train inexorably rose as the date approached, it was becoming increasingly difficult to keep a lid on the secret. After lengthy discussions between Matthew Golton and the Royal Household, it was finally agreed to release limited information about the train, and when they did, the reaction amongst enthusiasts was a stunned silence too.

Steam Railway trumpeted the news loudly, but it still seemed like a late April fool – this wasn't really possible, was it? The stakes were high – steam had been put under the microscope before, but nothing like this. A successful run would be good for the whole preservation movement, and could open doors for further high-profile operations in this vein. But if even a minor problem delayed the train, or if the tens of thousands of anticipated observers caused trouble, it could set back main-line steam operation for years. It really was that significant.

Duchess of Sutherland's last main-line operation before the Royal Train was on 11 May when she hauled a special from Leicester to Scarborough. When she returned to Swanwick on 13 May, the intensive preparations to get the engine in perfect condition started. The support coach 99041 was placed in 'quarantine' 11 days before the event while British Transport Police officers thoroughly searched it in case of explosives. Ceiling panels were removed and seats lifted before they were satisfied there was no danger to the royal party.

The support coach was repainted in LMS Crimson Lake to match the locomotive – repainting in the Royal Plum livery used on the Royal Train was forbidden – and the locomotive was given thorough boiler examinations and mechanical checks at the end of May to prove her fitness to run. At the start of June, extensive checks were made on the braking systems, and on 8 June *Duchess of Sutherland* was hauled out of the shed for photographs to be taken. The fire was then lit and steam gently raised. The 'Duchess' would depart for Crewe on 10 June.

The plan was for *Duchess of Sutherland* to haul the support coach to Crewe, where she would be coaled, and then she would travel to Holyhead. From there, after filling the tender with water, she would head to Valley for overnight stabling. Nerves amongst everyone involved – perhaps even the unflappable Chris Hillyard – must have been jangling by now as the finishing touches were put to *Duchess of Sutherland*. The next morning could make or break her reputation, and that of all those who'd potentially put whole careers on the line to give steam this one chance.

Chapter Twenty-Five
Crowning Glory

The eleventh of June dawned bright and a beautiful British summer's day beckoned as *Duchess of Sutherland* prepared to make preservation history. The night before, the Queen and the Duke of Edinburgh had travelled on the Royal Train overnight, and were due in Holyhead at 0500, when *Duchess of Sutherland* would take over.

The Royal Train conjures up images of grand palaces on wheels, and that was certainly true of previous incarnations, but the current train, which entered service in 1977, is a much more understated affair. While carriages like those in the National Railway Museum from previous Royal Trains have beautiful inlaid gold and veneers, and ornate panelling and fittings, these carriages have much simpler interiors. It's not to say they're not extremely comfortable, because there's no way the railway or the Royal Household would settle for anything less, but the design is very understated. It's a simpler, more straightforward interior that fits modern expectations of royal travel much better than fussy, ornate designs.

To reach the Royal Train's maintenance shed at Wolverton, near Milton Keynes, involves a mazy drive around the site to the carriage shed. Inside, it is otherworldly. The carriages are so highly polished that you really can see your face in the paintwork, and the smell is one of oil, polish and varnish – like a luxury car garage but many times stronger.

The carriages are laid out like the old corridor coaches, or indeed a present-day sleeping coach, but there the comparisons end. There are bedrooms for the Royals, and for the members of the Royal Household, but they're not the grand suites you'd expect. The Private Secretary's quarters are a little smaller than those of the Royals, but the configuration is the same. A surprisingly high bed – the top of the mattress is perhaps three feet off the ground – a desk and a chair form the bedroom, while adjacent is a small bathroom with toilet, sink, shower and bath. Paintings from the royal art collection are on the walls. The bedrooms are functional rather than plush because in the normal order of things, not much time is spent in them.

In another coach is the Prince of Wales's study. The Queen and Duke of Edinburgh both have similar facilities, but visitors to Wolverton aren't allowed to see them. In the study is a patterned blue sofa, desk and some chairs, and the overall effect is light and spacious, but the area itself is only about half the size of the bar area on the Night Riviera sleeper train. These studies are where the Principals relax before and after their duties. There's a dining coach too, which is used to serve food to Principals and guests, but again, the décor is very simple and understated. The Birds Eye Maple used throughout the train gives it a light feel, but the only gold trim you'll find is on a set of crockery and cutlery from the 1902 Royal Train, something kept for special occasions.

That the Royals are fond of the train is shown by some of

the railway memorabilia in it. Amongst it is an oversized Senior Citizen's Railcard presented to the Duke of Edinburgh in 1987, and the fifth ceremonial headlamp ordered for the day would also find a home inside the train. I've always felt that the Royal Train epitomises the best that Britain's railways can do, and having lost the yacht *Britannia*, I think it's really important that we keep and treasure this unique train. It's very much a functional, straightforward home on wheels for the Royal Family – but it's definitely not the palace you might imagine.

It's unlikely that Brell Ewart and Howard Routledge would have been considering the relative merits of the train's interior design when they started preparing *Duchess of Sutherland* at 0200 that morning for the locomotive's 0318 departure to Holyhead. Rather, they were preparing the fire and ensuring everything on No. 6233 was as ready as it possibly could be. As dawn broke, *Duchess of Sutherland* eased out of Valley to Holyhead, where, after running round her support coach, the tender was topped up with water. She was ready and waiting just outside the station when the Royal Train arrived with its two diesels (one as a spare in case the other failed) at Holyhead spot on time.

The locomotive and support coach now had to be coupled to the Royal Train as gently as possible as Her Majesty was sleeping just two coaches away from where the coupling would take place. Doing it without undue bumping is a real art that demands an intuitive understanding of the loco-motive and train and delicate but precise hands on regulator and brakes. The coupling was overseen by the man in charge of the Royal Train, Norman Pattenden MBE, and the first two attempts were too gentle as the couplers failed to engage. On the third try, with just a little more 'oomph' they were successful, and it was still done gently enough to avoid waking the sleeping Royals. Once the brakes had been tested to ensure they were working throughout the train, all was ready for departure.

Departure was at 0542, and Driver Graham Massey was in charge of the regulator. Easing it open gently, he managed a perfect start with no jolting, and gentle acceleration. There were anxious glances from the support coach at this, as the 1-in-75 gradient out of Holyhead station was a notorious slipping place in steam days, and on this duty even a small slip could be a black mark against the locomotive. Gradually speed rose, and *Duchess of Sutherland* got to grips with her heavy load, the exhaust quickening as speed quickly increased to 50mph before Massey shut off and coasted into Valley sidings, where the Queen would wake and breakfast, at walking pace. With two Principals on board, security stepped up a notch, and activity around the locomotive was kept to the bare minimum. A relief crew formed of Driver Bob Morrison, Fireman Bob Hart, Brian Radford and David Ward passed through the security and entered the support coach. The relief crew would take over from Massey, Fireman Eddie Williamson and traction inspector Jim Smith at Bangor.

On the dot of 0900, the diesel that was accompanying the train, No. 47 787 *Windsor Castle*, started up, and that was the signal for *Duchess of Sutherland* to be prepared for departure at 0918. A few minutes late, the diesel pulled the train backwards to gain access to the main line, stopping it just behind the starting signal at Valley station. It was now time for *Duchess of Sutherland* to show what she could do.

The departure on the main line was delayed by the Holyhead-London express running six minutes late. It is railway and Royal Household policy that the Royal Train should not be given precedence over service trains, and in the cab of *Duchess of Sutherland*, the support coach and the Royal Train itself, eyes flickered between watches and the timetable as the scarce recovery time built into the schedule was eaten up. Finally, at 0932 *Duchess of Sutherland* blew her whistle and headed to Llanfairpwll, the first stop. With much if not all of the recovery time gone, this tricky twenty-mile section had to be negotiated perfectly, but without exceeding the locomotive's 75mph speed limit. Massey had the bit between his teeth and smoothly opened the regulator. The locomotive responded like the thoroughbred she is, gathering speed easily despite the 501-ton load. As the train passed the golf course at RAF Valley, golfers raised their clubs to salute the train, and still speed increased to the maximum. The stations at Rhosneigr and Ty Croes were cruised past at speed. Through the tunnels at Bodorgan it went, until, two miles before Llanfairpwll, Massey shut off the regulator and allowed the train to coast, gently braking as the station approached. Despite the earlier delay, the train was now running early, and Massey slowed it to walking pace past the longest station name sign in the world (Llanfairpwllgwyngyll-gogerychwyrndrobwll-llantysilio-gogogoch). A thousand people were on the platform, and, to the strains of 'Men of Harlech', Massey stopped the train perfectly, the large double doors the Queen would exit from positioned in exactly the right place. *Duchess of Sutherland* had covered the twenty miles in seventeen minutes from a standing start with a load that wouldn't have looked out of place in a 1950s timetable ('a superlative piece of driving,' said Matthew Golton) – the day that had dawned so brightly was just getting better and better.

At Llanfairpwll, the royal party went by road to Beaumaris Castle, and the train carried on to Bangor, from where a BBC reporter and her crew who had been on the footplate were escorted off the locomotive and onto the platform. From Bangor the train retraced its steps back to Holyhead, the diesel locomotive at the rear of the train taking the load, and the relief crew took over, Driver Morrison at the regulator. The opportunity was taken to replenish *Duchess of Sutherland*'s tender and clean the fire. From Holyhead, *Duchess of Sutherland* would haul the Royal Train to Llandudno Junction, where she would haul the Queen and Duke of Edinburgh as far as Crewe. This time there was no rush to get to the next calling point, as the train was due to arrive there at 1402, in time for a two-hour layover in which *Duchess of Sutherland* would receive a final quick clean.

The scene at Llandudno Junction was epic – every vantage point was packed, with crowd barriers along the length of the platform, and a special press pen set up for the media to record the Queen and the Duke of Edinburgh boarding their first steam-hauled Royal Train for thirty-five years. Anticipation rose to fever pitch as the Queen's 1615 arrival time neared, and a presentation party formed of railway and Royal Train staff, dignitaries and representatives from the PRCLT lined up. As the Queen and the Duke of Edinburgh passed the presentation party, the Duke talked to David Ward and Brian Radford, and expressed surprise and delight at the speed of the run from Valley to Llanfairpwll. He asked Morrison if he was responsible for the run: Morrison, with superlative honesty, credited Massey with it. The Duke was soon joined by the Queen, who also commented on the quality of the run to Llanfairpwll. To everyone's surprise, as they were running a few minutes early, the royal pair took the opportunity to talk to the support crew of No. 6233, something that will live long in the memories of all involved. Brell Ewart presented Her Majesty with the fifth commemorative headlamp, showed her and the Duke the front of the locomotive and the headboard, and then the royal party boarded the train.

Departure from Llandudno Junction was delayed after liaison between Railtrack control and Norman Pattenden, and three minutes before the rearranged departure time, the train went on its way. If there was any doubt about the popularity of the monarchy, or of the effect the train had, it was blown away by the crowds. People were everywhere they could possibly be – on bridges, on stations and in fields and roads along the route – nothing like this had been seen for years, both the train itself and the crowds on the lineside.

Duchess of Sutherland's performance was every bit as good as earlier, keeping to time perfectly. A nice side effect of the delay was that rather than having to pause in a loop line to allow a service train to pass, the train was now running exactly to the time it would have been had it waited there. Speed was eased on the approach to Chester, which was passed a minute early. The crews and Royal Train staff must have been exhilarated, but all good things come to an end, and as Crewe was approached, speed was gently cut as *Duchess of Sutherland* passed her birthplace and entered Platform 12 at Crewe a minute and a half early. This platform was chosen because of its isolation from the rest of the station, making security easier even at the price of denying a view to the crowds. Her Majesty came to the double doors to thank the crews, delighted at the experience, and of course, by the tens, if not hundreds, of thousands who had thronged the lineside to watch the train pass.

Chris Hillyard presented Brell Ewart with a plaque marking the event, and then *Duchess of Sutherland* headed south to turn on the triangle at Gresty Lane and Basford Hall. Quick work by the signallers meant that she was able to pass the Royal Train on the adjacent track, and did so at walking pace. The Queen came to the windows of her saloon and offered a more private thanks to the footplate crew. The Duke of Edinburgh, in his own saloon next to the Queen's, leant out of the window with a huge smile on his face, obviously enjoying every minute of the trip. *Duchess of Sutherland* headed to Crewe Heritage Centre for servicing, while a diesel took over to haul the train south for overnight stabling. An amazing day was over.

Ewart said afterwards that he didn't have any butterflies: 'I don't allow myself to get on tenterhooks – but I've lain in bed and gone through the fine detail of the arrangements so many times in the last few weeks that I was sure our planning and preparation was as thorough as it could have been. There's no legislating for mechanical failure, but I think we got our homework right.'

Matthew Golton's faith in the PRCLT had been repaid, and then some: 'I've been hugely impressed with the thoroughly professional approach the PRCLT has taken from day one. It's been a really well-knitted team effort, and a pleasure to work with them.'

John Riley was one of the volunteers I met at Crewe and he was a key member of the support crew on the day. 'It was a relief it all went well,' he said, but the day meant much more for him. 'I was proud for all the people involved, and that everything went to plan. It was good for preservation as a whole.'

John was right – this epic, fairy-tale run had placed steam preservation in particular, and railway preservation in general, right in the spotlight. For such an old machine to be entrusted with such a prestigious duty, and with such tight timings, was something that must have given any number of people sleepless nights, but everything went to plan, and *Duchess of Sutherland* answered every question asked of her that day. The fillip she gave preservation simply cannot be undervalued – after all, she now had royal approval.

Chapter Twenty-Six
Sublime *Sutherland*

O f course, around *Duchess of Sutherland*'s Royal Train duties, she continued her main-line duties, and rapidly took on *Duchess of Hamilton*'s mantle as one of the pre-eminent steam locomotives passed for main-line running. She proved as able as one would expect on her first few runs, but her best wasn't to come until later. Before then, she had a date at the Severn Valley Railway in Shropshire, where her boiler had been repaired.

The Severn Valley's Autumn Steam Galas bring a collection of locomotives from around the country to join the line's home fleet for a weekend of intensive and varied running, and over the years they have become one of the 'must visit' events in the enthusiast calendar, but the gala of autumn 2001 was special. The star of the show was *Duchess of Sutherland*, returning to the railway complete and ready to show what she could do. Although the Severn Valley, at sixteen miles, is one of Britain's longest heritage railways, the economics of running a big locomotive like a 'Duchess' mean that, generally speaking, it is preferable to run smaller locomotives such as 'Black 5s'. This is because even though only a fraction of the power of a 'Duchess' is needed, you can't leave half the firegrate uncovered to compensate, so just to keep a 'Duchess' standing still in steam means you might need a couple of tons of coal, and when you start running one, the bill mounts further. This is why even on this line, which runs some of the longest trains in preservation, a visit by a 'Duchess' is something to be savoured. And it was. Never mind that no 'Duchesses' ever ran on the route while it was operated by BR, or that with a blanket 25mph limit (the same as applies to all heritage railways) *Duchess of Sutherland* would be unable to stretch her legs, the spectacle of the locomotive amongst all the authentically restored infrastructure was like time travel, and thanks to the SVR's rake of LMS coaches, it was the first time the locomotive had been paired in LMS livery with carriages in the same style for more than half a century – it was a wonderful weekend that many will long remember.

The Severn Valley Gala, as wonderful as it was, was a rare visit to a heritage railway by *Duchess of Sutherland*, and as crews once again got used to driving and firing a 'Duchess' on the main line, she won a new set of admirers, and 27 October 2001's 'The Mayflower' from Bristol to Plymouth finally laid the ghost of *City of Bradford*'s performances during the Locomotive Exchanges to rest. Despite the ferocious Devon banks between Plymouth and Exeter, she managed to keep time with a heavy load of ten coaches, and then gained seven minutes on the return leg from Exeter to Bristol, the crew agreeing that she had plenty in hand. It was becoming clear that there could be some fabulous performances in the future.

And they came sooner than expected, and appropriately, in the run-up to the Royal Train in 2002. On 20 April that year, *Duchess of Sutherland* returned to do battle with Shap for the first time since the 1960s, and Mike Notley was on the train, eagerly timing it. He reckoned 1,850hp at the drawbar was recorded before Preston, and hoped for great things, with Driver Bill Andrew at the regulator.

The initial climb of Grayrigg to Oxenholme was described by Notley as 'measured', the intention being to get *Duchess of Sutherland* ready for the stiff climb. Speed restrictions meant that it wasn't until Milepost 27¼ that Andrew was able to give *Sutherland* the gun, and by the start of the real climbing, at Milepost 31½, *Duchess of Sutherland* was running in the mid-70s, the maximum speed she was allowed. As the gradient steepened to 1-in-75, she was still doing 73mph, and after the first mile 65mph. With just 1.5 miles to go until the summit, she was doing 56mph, but then the brakes were applied gently by someone apparently pulling a communication cord in the train, bringing her down to 48mph at the summit. Notley was miffed: 'But for the braking, it might have been so much better. The "Duchesses" don't give the feeling that they are working hard and I have to admit that my immediate impression was of a good but not record [in preservation] climb. It just goes to show how wrong you can be! Our time had clipped almost four seconds off the previous preservation best despite the braking which had cost us around 7 sec over the final mile.'

Notley was surprised by this, and when he found out that she'd done it at a maximum cut-off of 35% – perhaps equivalent to fourth gear in a car and meaning that *Duchess of Sutherland* was never even put into the steam equivalent of second or first gear – he was even more so. So huge were *Duchess of Sutherland*'s reserves of power that she simply didn't need to be thrashed over the hills. This policy, which would be continued on future runs with the locomotive, is an extremely sensible one for an elderly locomotive, however powerful. By deliberately not thrashing her and trying to set records, the wear and tear caused by high-speed main-line running is kept to a minimum, and that's good for everyone as the chances of expensive repair bills and expensive failures on the main line are kept to a minimum.

After her Royal Train run in 2002, *Duchess of Sutherland* continued enthralling thousands of passengers and lineside observers, and the following summer she was able to expand her throng of admirers at a big open day at Crewe Works. Open days at railway works had long been a regular fixture, the railway companies and then BR showing off their flagship trains and heritage locomotives to raise money for charity. On the weekend of 31 May and 1 June 2003, some 30,000 people visited Crewe Works, and the stars of the show were two Stanier 'Pacifics', *Duchess of Sutherland* and No. 6201 *Princess Elizabeth*, Stanier's second 'Pacific' and the predecessor of the 'Duchesses'. *Sutherland* looked magnificent, complete with Royal Train headboard, a suitable flagship for an event at her birthplace. The following year, she would do battle with Shap again, and set yet another new record for preserved steam on that demanding section. Again, Mike Notley was on board on 4 September 2004. Notley has pretty much seen it all when it comes to main-line steam operation, and it takes a lot to impress him, but on that day, even this hard-nosed train timer couldn't help but admire the locomotive's performance.

After a blistering climb of Grayrigg, some locomotives

can be winded, and need time for the fireman to get the fire back on track, but not this time. 'Today there were no such worries,' wrote Notley in *Steam Railway*, 'and as we immediately picked up speed, I admit to getting rather over-emotional. A travelling companion was at the opposite window in the vestibule end, and as we swept under the motorway bridge and half a mile beyond the top of Grayrigg, he shouted across that we'd soon know what state she was in.

'I looked forward from the ninth coach and saw a pure white exhaust streaming back over the coaches. Then, another plume of steam began to rise, this time from the safety valves. "My God, she's feathering," I shouted back, and I have to admit to a lump in my throat as I watched this majestic locomotive doing just what she was designed to do and so obviously on top of the job.'

I can empathise with Notley. On the face of it, it might seem daft to get emotional about a steam locomotive, but a performance like that, and with so much in hand, is something akin to the last night of the Proms. With the noise from the chimney combining with the sound of lifting safety valves, and the roar of the train, it was, to use a rail enthusiast cliché, a symphony of steam, and if your ear is tuned to such things, it was beautiful: sometimes things are so good, that it brings a lump to your throat and a tear to your eye. With twelve coaches behind, *Duchess of Sutherland* stormed Shap in 5 min 52 secs, a record with such a load in preservation, and the fourth fastest with any load. Notley calculated the maximum horsepower at 2,000, suggesting that, once again, the locomotive had plenty in hand.

Unsurprisingly, Mike Notley has been following the

locomotive closely, and his verdict is that she has been wisely managed and, with a few exceptions, has rarely been asked any serious questions. 'The words "easy competence" often spring to mind when discussing her performances as she goes about her work in an efficient manner, only occasionally deigning to break into an unseemly sweat,' he told me.

Notley reckons her finest performance in preservation wasn't the Shap record or the Royal Train, but was on 23 July 2005 when she stood in for the unavailable 'A4' No. 60009 *Union of South Africa* on 'The Talisman' tour from King's Cross to Darlington and back. This involved hauling a thirteen-coach, 505-ton load over 465 miles against a tight schedule on a busy main line where any slip-ups would be very disruptive and seriously damaging as far as steam's reputation was concerned.

At the end of a long and exciting day, steam's reputation was not only intact, it was enhanced and we had enjoyed one of the great steam runs *of all time* [Notley's italics]. 6233 had produced three mile-a-minute start-to-stop runs, a demand-ing feat considering her 75mph speed limit. The first was between King's Cross and Peterborough, a distance of 76.35 miles, which she covered at an average speed of 60.6mph. The second and third were on the famous speedway that is the York to Darlington stretch. On the way north, it was covered at an average speed of 64mph, while in the opposite direction it was even higher, at 66.1mph.

This wasn't simply the best run in preservation by some margin; it was a run that was of historical significance as far as the class and steam in general were concerned. *Duchess of Sutherland* and her crews of Driver Bill Andrew and Fireman Alastair Meanley northbound and Driver Ron Smith and Fireman Graeme Bunker southbound had between them crafted one of the great steam runs of all time.

A few weeks later, *Duchess of Sutherland* was in the news again, this time replacing the National Railway Museum's icon No. 4472 *Flying Scotsman* to take Prime Minister Tony Blair to open the museum's outstation at Shildon. *Flying Scotsman* had failed, and the museum wouldn't rush the repairs and risk the locomotive. The success of the Royal Train two years before meant that the Prime Minister could have no qualms about travelling behind steam, and although *Duchess of Sutherland* wasn't the first choice, as she wasn't owned by the NRM, she did the job, as usual to perfection. It seemed that travelling behind *Duchess of Sutherland* was becoming, if not de rigueur, then at least perfectly acceptable because in 2005, despite assertions back in 2002 that the steam-hauled Royal Train was likely to be a one-off, *Duchess of Sutherland* was due to haul Prince Charles, and there was even talk that he'd have a go 'on the shovel'.

The occasion was a visit by the Prince of Wales on 22 March to functions at Kirkby Stephen and Appleby, both stations on the scenic Settle–Carlisle line that *Duchess of Hamilton* dominated in the 1980s and 1990s. The Prince, always appreciative of good architecture and fine scenery, had said he wanted to visit the line, and if possible to do so behind steam – there were no guesses as to which locomotive would be chosen! The last time he'd been hauled by steam on the Royal Train was thought to have been in 1962.

The day before, similar preparations to those of 2002 took place, but this time at Hellifield, near Skipton. On this day, the Royal Train had travelled overnight, and arrived at Clapham, on the Preston–Settle line, where Prince Charles left the train to start his duties. The Royal Train continued to Hellifield for No. 6233 to take over. Gently, *Duchess of Sutherland* and her support coach coupled to the train and eased onto the line heading for Settle, where the Prince would rejoin it. All the stations on the line were decked out with decorations, and local people, schoolkids and bands were all there to mark the occasion.

At Settle, the train stopped with the Prince of Wales's saloon right opposite him, enabling him to board quickly and easily. Fireman Brian Grierson was busy building the fire for the climbing ahead, and Driver John Finlinson of Carlisle got the train moving on the 1-in-100 gradient. Crowds gathered at vantage points all along the line while Prince Charles hosted railway staff on the run to Kirkby Stephen. It took a while for *Duchess of Sutherland* to get warmed up and although there was recovery time in the schedule, it wouldn't do to use any. The train slowed for the spectacular twenty-four-arch Ribblehead Viaduct (one of the prime reasons stated for the line's proposed closure in the 1980s), and the train arrived in Kirkby Stephen eleven seconds late, within the plus or minus fifteen-second window the train operates to.

At Kirkby Stephen, Prince Charles opened the newly refurbished station buildings and then met the train crew and Brell Ewart, the chairman of the PRCLT, for his footplate ride to Appleby. It was the PRCLT that persuaded him to have a footplate ride. 'Riding on the footplate of a crack express locomotive like *Duchess of Sutherland* on the Settle to Carlisle line is really the ultimate steam experience so we suggested to the Prince's office at Clarence House that he might like to join us in the cab for a spell,' Ewart told David Wilcock. 'Obviously we hoped he'd say yes – but we were bowled over by the enthusiasm of the response we got. He was really keen to see the locomotive at close quarters and very obviously enjoyed himself.'

The Prince dressed appropriately for this part of the journey in a blue serge 'traction inspector's coat and greasetop cap', but he declined to have a go at firing. 'I really oughtn't to,' he said. 'I've got a bad back.' Fireman Grierson then risked a remark that many years ago could have won him a rather-too-close haircut by replying, 'I've got a bad back too – but I've still got to fire the thing all the way to Carlisle!'

At Appleby, Prince Charles left the footplate and visited the waiting room and Friends of the Settle–Carlisle Line shop before reboarding the train for the final run to Carlisle. Arrival at Carlisle's train shed saw a band of Scottish pipers strike up to mark the Royal Train's arrival, and the Prince walked down the platform to thank the train crew and PRCLT's ever-dedicated support crew, where he was presented with an engraved shovel by one of the Trust's youngest volunteers, thirteen-year-old Adam Miles, to mark his run.*

---

* *Prince Charles is making a habit of steam-hauled Royal Trains – on 10 June 2008, the Royal Train visited the Severn Valley Railway to mark its reopening, by Prince Charles and the Duchess of Cornwall. This time, he took the regulator of the steam locomotive, No. 6024 King Edward I, for a short distance between Bewdley and Arley.*

Duchess of Sutherland was due to be withdrawn from traffic in late 2009 with the expiry of its boiler certificate, but the days of rigid 10-year 'tickets' have been superseded in favour of a condition-based regime which offered the potential for No. 6233 to operate a little longer.

The PRCLT was confident its policy of operating the locomotive relatively gently and ensuring it was always kept in tip-top condition would pay off and following detailed inspections of the locomotive's condition a 12-month extension to its boiler certificate was granted.

In its final year of operation before withdrawal for a comprehensive overhaul, *Duchess of Sutherland* was painted in the LMS lined black livery it carried after the Second World War. In black the locomotive loses a little of its gloss and glamour but none of its muscular appearance, and it has been a unique spectacle on the rails in its final few months of service.

When she does finally head back to Butterley for overhaul, for the first time in a decade there will be no 'Duchess' on the main line - but it's a case of au revoir rather than goodbye. With any luck it won't be too long before we see her at the head of a main line charter train once more.

Chapter Twenty-Seven

Streamliner!

Duchess of Hamilton was placed on display at York in 1998 after spending the two years left on her boiler certificate touring preserved railways. In December the year before, she had been painted in BR green at the East Lancashire Railway, but on her return to York was repainted back into the Crimson Lake that suited her so well. The 229 Club, a group devoted to raising funds for the locomotive's overhaul, considered its next move.

The supporters had long wanted to reinstate the streamlining on *Duchess of Hamilton*, almost from when the locomotive arrived at York. They were well aware that *City of Birmingham* represented a genuine 1960s example, and that *Duchess of Sutherland* was showing what a non-streamlined 'Duchess' looked like in LMS days – but there were no streamlined 'Duchesses', a significant gap in railway preservation and one that would complete the set of three 'Duchesses'. *Duchess of Hamilton* had lost her streamlining at the beginning of 1948.

It wasn't until 1998, just after *Duchess of Sutherland*'s Lottery grant came through, that things started moving. The 229 Club issued a press statement reminding people that plans for that locomotive's return to steam would be announced in September, the sixtieth anniversary of the locomotive, offering the tantalising possibility of seeing two 'Duchesses' in action on the main line. It surprised nobody that both groups were delighted at this. After *Sutherland*'s turn in the limelight, a stunning announcement was to be made in September about *Duchess of Hamilton*.

Forty-nine years before, No. 46243 *City of Lancaster* had been the last 'Duchess' to have her streamlining removed, but now a bold joint venture was set to return *Duchess of Hamilton* to the main line with the classic streamlining on. The deal was made between the National Railway Museum, the owner of *Duchess of Hamilton*, and Venice-Simplon Orient Express (VSOE), which operated luxury trains in Britain and abroad, including the 'Orient Express'. VSOE was looking for a locomotive to haul trains in the north of England, and a streamlined *Duchess of Hamilton* would make a perfect subject. The locomotive would appear in her original LMS Crimson Lake livery (though VSOE originally wanted blue, something it later changed its mind about) at the head of a train in matching colours – a modern-day LMS streamliner if you will.

This was exciting stuff – and it looked like it was a near-certainty too. VSOE – then owned by Sea Containers – had the resources to make the overhaul happen, but there would be a sting in the tail for enthusiasts unable to afford the prices of luxury dining trains. Though *Duchess of Hamilton* would be nominally available for other work when she wasn't hauling the luxury trains, it was estimated that there would only be around five slots a year for lower-priced enthusiast specials. It raised the question of whether a locomotive owned by the public should be used on such duties, which would inevitably restrict access to all bar those with money to spend.

The contract for the rebuilding of *Duchess of Hamilton* was due to be signed in summer 1999, but when it was, it wasn't for the overhaul: it was for an engineering assessment to establish costs. However, just a few months later, VSOE put the deal on hold as it said it wanted to study the implications of the Ladbroke Grove crash, near London, on 5 October 1999. VSOE maintained that the money was there, but that 'it would be foolish of us to invest a lot of money in the "Duchess" and then find there is something in the accident report which inhibits our plans for running it.' It seemed likely that new safety equipment designed to stop trains passing red signals would have to be installed, and there were concerns about the cost, and of whether installing sophisticated modern safety systems in a steam locomotive was even possible. By March 2000, the deal was officially dead, after VSOE passed a deadline to confirm its investment. It was a sad end to an exciting project, but after firing people's imaginations, it would resurface a few years later in an altogether different form.

With the collapse of this scheme, things rested for a little while, but the 229 Club still wanted to reinstate the streamlining on *Duchess of Hamilton* and was still raising money to support the locomotive. One benefit of VSOE's aborted bid was that they now had a thorough understanding of the locomotive's condition and the work that would be required, and it would have been a shame if this was wasted. In 2004, the ambitions took a huge step forward, when the 229 Club contacted *Steam Railway* magazine to see if its readers would be willing to raise the last £25,000 or so needed to return No. 6229 to her original condition: if the appeal was successful, the project was a goer.

The 229 Club's chairman, Don Heath, said, 'There are no plans whatsoever at this stage to return the locomotive to the main line but we will do nothing to prevent this happening when the circumstances are right.'

Steam Railway's then editor, Tony Streeter, had considered the appeal very carefully before agreeing to help. 'We thought it was a very exciting project, and potentially well worth doing, but we were also aware that perceptions among our readers might not be as clear-cut as with other appeals we'd launched.'

After careful consideration, Streeter thought that re-streamlining *Duchess of Hamilton would* spark his readers' imagination – and decided that his magazine would give all the help and support it could to the 229 Club and NRM.

The work required was extensive, with new cladding for the locomotive sides, a new smokebox, cladding and doors, a new chimney and bufferbeam, and of course support brackets for the casing. The tender also needed extensions to its side plates and skirting to return it to streamlined condition. In December 2004, a further study was commissioned at a project meeting in York, which saw re-streamlining *Duchess of Hamilton* given the green light. It was helped by Birmingham Railway Museum's Chief Engineer, Bob Meanley, who is an unashamed fan of the streamlined 'Duchesses': 'When I was a spotter at Tamworth in the 1950s, all anyone ever said to me was that I should have seen the "Coronation Scot". That was 20 years later – and in a town where it never even stopped!' he said.

Steam Railway, together with the NRM and the 229 Club, launched an appeal to raise the missing £25,000 it was thought was needed, and very quickly donations started pouring in, with £10,000 raised days after the magazine hit the newsstands. A series of incentives were offered to supporters, including the chance to see *Duchess of Hamilton* unstreamlined but with the sloping smokebox many 'Duchesses' ran with after the streamlining was removed, for people who donated £150 or more to the appeal. A further plan was to display the locomotive at an open day at Crewe planned for 10–11 September 2005. After that, *Duchess of Hamilton* would be towed to Tyseley, Birmingham, where Bob Meanley and his team could install the streamlining. At the time, Meanley reckoned it could be done by November 2006, subject to a clear run and no problems being found.

Duchess of Hamilton was towed to Crewe by rail for a reunion of four of the five surviving Stanier 'Pacifics' at another open weekend. Joining her were the PRCLT's No. 6203 *Princess Margaret Rose*, a non-runner, and *Duchess of Sutherland*, which was continuing to demonstrate her power and speed on the main line. Completing the quartet was No. 6201 *Princess Elizabeth*. It was the first time in preservation that these four locomotives, which had been based together at Camden sixty years before, had been reunited and tens of thousands of people gathered to see this line-up. It was a great opportunity to promote the plan to re-streamline *Duchess of Hamilton*, and a lot of support was drummed up. After the open weekend at Crewe, *Duchess of Hamilton* was hauled behind a diesel to Tyseley, and then Meanley and crew could get their teeth into this exciting project.

By the end of October, the funding gap was just £7,000, and Don Heath explained why he thought the project was so important to Tony Streeter.

'*Duchess of Hamilton* came out of operation in 1998 and, whilst it's a wonderful static exhibit, it is vital to do things to keep interest in the engine alive. Streamlining immediately makes it very different and will create something fantastic that is bound to hit a real chord with the public and enthusiasts. The engine will dominate everything else in the museum – even *Mallard*.'

But Heath reckoned the benefits of streamlining could be even greater. The NRM, like any railway, can only restore and operate a given number of locomotives at a time, and *Duchess of Hamilton* was a long way down the list. Streamlining her, reckoned Heath, would push her back up the list of priorities. A month later, at the end of November, the fundraising appeal had hit the £25,000 target, with donations still coming in. The only question now was when we would see her as the LMS intended.

Before that could happen, one of the commitments made to supporters was fulfilled on 6 May 2006, when, after much work – all connected directly with the streamlining, *Duchess of Hamilton* was painted in LMS black complete with sloping smokebox. For many spotters in the 1940s and 1950s, this was what a 'Duchess' should look like, and for a day or so, those who'd put £150 or more to the appeal were able to relive old memories. The work involved cutting off the conventional cylindrical smokebox top and replacing the door ring with one the correct shape to match the streamlined casing that would eventually cover it. It was done in great secrecy in Tyseley to surprise the supporters, and there was a further surprise in store. *Duchess of Hamilton* arrived at Tyseley in Crimson Lake, but former Derby Works painter Ernie Bradley painted the left-hand side of the locomotive in black, complete with correct lettering, numbering and lining – and donated his fee to the appeal. The locomotive looked absolutely spectacular, the modifications not denting the impression of power a bit. It was the first time since the 1960s that a locomotive had been seen with this type of smokebox, and it was a just reward for all the supporters.

At Tyseley work was moving rapidly on *Duchess of Hamilton*'s tender to give it the characteristic fairings on the sides, and in September 2006 it was finally completed, the first streamlined 'Duchess' tender for years. It meant that Bob Meanley and his team could concentrate on the locomotive, but it was more difficult than a layman might imagine: 'When people look at photographs of streamlined "Coronations" they tend to think the form is fairly simple, but in reality there are barely two panels the same shape on the whole thing.

'Nobody's fitted streamlining to a "Coronation" for over 60 years so we're working forward piece by piece ensuring each is right. It's a bit like eating an elephant – you have to do it in bite-sized chunks!'

Meanley's caution was well placed, as even if they followed the engineering drawings exactly, differences between the locomotives when they were built (and they were all, essentially, hand-built) meant that mounting points and spacings for support brackets and the like could be slightly different on *Duchess of Hamilton*. And this proved to be the case, not helped by the fact that many of the crucial drawings are missing. Meanley visited the successor to Birmingham Museum of Science and Industry, Thinktank, to examine *City of Birmingham* for clues to help. Amongst modifications undertaken when *Duchess of Hamilton* was de-streamlined in 1948 was the addition of an access door in the footplating to allow easier access to the outside cylinders. This had to be replaced with a solid plate.

In early 2007, work was making good progress, though rather later than anticipated, and the first casing panels were fitted below the cab and on the footplate, and as the year continued, bit by bit the pieces came together. At the end of the year the curved front doors, the most difficult and complex part of the streamlining to make, were taking shape at Coventry Prototype Panels, which normally makes panels for prototype sports cars. Completing the door skins was one thing, but installing the supporting brackets was quite another. The angle irons have to be bent by hand through a constantly changing angle to fit correctly – that Tyseley is able to do this speaks volumes of its craftsmanship. Other work completed by this time included the new chimney, and all the valancing on the tender.

Far from being completed in 2006 or 2007, *Duchess of Hamilton* still wasn't complete at the start of 2008, though this was nothing to do with funds or the team at Tyseley. Re-streamlining the 'Duchess' to as close to original condition as possible depended on finding steel sheets of the correct dimensions, and this was proving a considerable challenge. Other than the side cladding, restoration work was very nearly complete, but without it, the project would remain unfinished. Meanley had been seeking these sheets for a long time, but their dimensions of 3,000mm x 2,000mm and 1.5mm thick posed a problem. His investigations suggested that all supplies in the UK came from 1,500mm wide coils. The hunt now went global. Salvation seemed to come when eighteen sheets were found in Australia, but they were found to be 3mm thick – far too bulky for the 'Duchess'. At the time of writing, just one supplier had been found, in China, but the drawback was that a bulk order of 1,000 tons would be required. As Meanley says, 'Unless we decide to build a fleet of 1,000 streamlined 'Princess Coronations' that could probably be considered as a little uneconomic.' And there things remained stalled for around 12 months. Meanley continued his search for the correct steel but the results were the same: it simply wasn't economic for the world's steel manufacturers to deliver the relatively small quantities needed for the restreamlining of *Duchess of Hamilton*.

Then, in August 2008 a dramatic intervention found a solution. Baron Snape of Wednesbury, the former MP for West Bromwich, spoke of the locomotive's plight to the Personal Private Secretary to then Prime Minister Gordon Brown, a man called Ian Austin. Austin approached a senior board member at Corus' parent company TATA in India through the British High Commission. Events moved quickly and special authorisation was granted for Corus South Wales to produce a special batch of the steel so desperately needed.

Meanley was grateful, having begun to seriously consider using aluminium or welding smaller steel sections together. 'Neither of these would have been at all satisfactory,' he said, adding: 'We owe a debt of thanks to TATA, Corus and the members of government involved for exhibiting such joined up thinking. Now we will have original specification steel, so it will be done once and done right.'

Once the steel arrived in Autumn 2008, Meanley and his team wasted little time in cutting it and shaping it to 'Hamilton's new form. From December that year the big 'Pacific' underwent the final stages of its metamorphosis. By January 21, when contributors to the streamlining appeal were invited to see progress, the locomotive was only 12 weeks away from completion.

The complications of the project meant that costs rose above forecast and a £40,000 funding gap was the result. A final push to raise the funds was successful and in Spring 2009 the last remaining job was completion of the paintwork. Master Signwriter Bob Timmins took an original sample of LMS crimson pigment to J&L Industrial Paints of Weston-super-Mare for them to replicate as he felt contamination of the original LMS paint swatch held in the National Railway Museum meant that its accuracy couldn't be trusted.

Timmins and his son Ralph applied the new and accurate coach enamel before embarking on the daunting task of applying around a quarter of a mile each of black and vermillion lining, as well as 320ft of 1 1/8 inch and 5 inch thick gold lines – all applied by hand under demanding conditions and a tight deadline.

The result was stunning – a beautiful crimson and gold-lined streamlined 'Duchess' ready for its final move to York.

Duchess of Hamilton returned to its home at the National Railway Museum in York on 18 May 2009, hauled from

Tyseley by a Class 47 diesel. For the first time in decades, a streamlined 'Duchess' graced the tracks of the national network, and confounded those sceptics who believed the locomotive's appearance would be ruined. Resting in the Great Hall of the NRM, 'Hamilton' looks as stunning as the rest of us had hoped she would, and helps complete the story of that great locomotive arms race of the 1930s which saw some of the finest machines ever built take to the rails. She won't steam in the near future, but surely, towards the end of the decade, it would be appropriate to launch an appeal to return her to traffic in her original form. That really would be the icing on the cake for this magnificent machine.

Chapter Twenty-Eight
Thinking Big

With *Duchess of Sutherland* continuing to run extremely well on the main line, and *Duchess of Hamilton* soon, we hope, to gain her side panels and have her streamlining completed, you could be forgiven for thinking that *City of Birmingham* has been forgotten, but nothing could be further from the truth. In the mid-1990s, when No. 46229 was eking out her boiler certificate, and the PRCLT was trying to raise funds for No. 6233, a bold plan to put *City of Birmingham* at the centre of a new museum in the city was starting to come to fruition.

Birmingham Museum of Science and Industry closed its doors for ever in 1997, as construction and fitting out of a new more spacious and modern facility called Thinktank started in earnest. The aim of the new museum was to better display and interpret the old one's exhibits, and to provide space for future acquisitions. In a city that produced almost every form of transport, the ground floor of Thinktank would be devoted to transport, and the two top exhibits were expected to be a Spitfire fighter plane built in the city, and *City of Birmingham*. The aircraft would be suspended from the ceiling, meaning that the museum's huge steam locomotive would take centre stage on the floor. The only problem was that she couldn't be moved there until

Thinktank was ready to take her – and, indeed, the building had to be completed around her once she had moved!

After four years of construction work, *City of Birmingham* was moved by road across the city centre – causing traffic chaos like she did in 1966 when she arrived! – to her new home. She bore a special 'Discovery Centre Trust Express' headboard to mark the move. The locomotive was to rest her 105-ton bulk, plus that of the tender, on specially strengthened foundations: it wouldn't do for a 'Duchess' to cause the museum to subside. She was stabled overnight on her road trailer while the track from the old museum was carefully transferred to her final resting place. Then she was winched into the new museum onto her tracks. Only then could the frontage be completed and the museum opened.

It's tempting, given how little publicity *City of Birmingham* attracts, to believe that she's been forgotten, and while that might be true for many enthusiasts, it's certainly not the case for the thousands of visitors to Thinktank. The locomotive has been separated from the tender and an accessible walkway built alongside the locomotive and between the gap to show the footplate and tender to best effect. It means visitors can very nearly place themselves in the driver's seat of a BR green steam locomotive circa 1964 and imagine what it must have been like back in the day. Surveys suggest it's gone down well. One female adult (this is how the museum labels its respondents!) put it succinctly: 'I don't particularly like trains, but thought *City of Birmingham* was beautiful!' And a young girl visiting expressed her surprise too: 'I think it is so big and thought it would be much smaller.'

Even Jack Kirkby, a man who knows his exhibits inside

out, admits to being flummoxed by *City of Birmingham*'s scale: 'You get used to seeing the locomotive, and sometimes you don't appreciate how big she is until you go into a room nearby and realise she couldn't possibly fit in there!'

There have been, and occasionally still are, periodic calls for *City of Birmingham* to be restored: *Steam World* described her as 'The Prisoner' in the 1980s, and in the course of researching this book I've seen similar descriptions elsewhere all referring to her captive and lifeless status, but it seems that finally her significance for what she is – a 'Duchess' overhauled by Crewe in 1966 – is being realised, and Kirkby agrees: 'It's reached a point where she's now being appreciated for her originality – she's almost a historical document.' And the argument is strong. She has original BR paint; the parts were all fitted in service (or perhaps overhauled, as we discussed earlier); you can see where the streamlining was removed if you know what to look for – something Bob Meanley valued greatly during the re-streamlining of *Duchess of Hamilton* – and so on. She's now a kind of memorial to the men who worked at Crewe during the last days of steam, and that's something worth conserving.

Aside from the practical difficulties of extracting her, would there be any value in steaming her anyway? She'd have to be altered to comply with modern regulations, and a lot of parts might need removal and replacing. In returning her to steam we'd be destroying historic material. For the other two 'Duchesses', that's not a matter of such great importance as original material was lost in the first restorations in the 1970s, and they have been altered with the likes of air brakes since then. With *Duchess of Hamilton* imminently streamlined, and *Duchess of Sutherland* running unstreamlined (she never was streamlined and she never will be), would running *City of Birmingham* tell us anything new? No.

Thinktank plans to shift the interpretation of *City of Birmingham* from its current social focus to one based much more on engineering and science. It won't happen for a few years, but already Jack Kirkby and the team there are considering interactive displays explaining how she works, and aspects of her design such as streamlining. Whatever happens, though, she will remain in Birmingham as a dearly loved and very popular exhibit at an absolutely fantastic museum.

Chapter Twenty-Nine
The Ultimate

So, what are we to make of the 'Duchesses', then – what is it that makes them Britain's ultimate steam locomotives?

Inevitably, one first looks to their huge power. The feats of *Duchess of Abercorn* in 1939, and of *Duchess of Hamilton* and *Duchess of Sutherland* in preservation, represent levels of steam locomotive performance that have never been matched in Britain, and that exceed all bar a select handful of diesel designs too. The 'Duchesses' were so powerful, in fact, that even today we don't know what their absolute technical limit is – as far as one can tell, if a fireman can get the coal in fast enough, a 'Duchess' will burn it effectively to generate more steam. That sort of power gives crews the confidence to push their engines when required, knowing that they'll be able to handle it.

Which brings me on to the second reason for their success because, as one car manufacturer once asserted, power is nothing without control. You can have all the power you like – 5,000hp, 10,000, 50,000 – but it's academic if the wheels spin round uselessly when you open the throttle. Driving a locomotive like a 'Duchess' is rather like driving a supercar without traction control, in that there's really too much power for it all to be put down on the rails at once. With locomotives of this size, there's a fine line between a locomotive being able to get a grip, or slipping to a stand, and the 'Duchesses' were pretty good in this respect. Factors such as weight distribution, the design of the regulator and valves, the valve gear itself – all play their part. Get it slightly wrong, as Oliver Bulleid did with his big 'Pacifics', and there can be some spectacular slips when you're trying to get away with a heavy load – sensitive hands were the order of the day with many designs.

Yet the 'Duchesses' always seemed much more tolerant of different driving styles than their counterparts elsewhere. Obviously, all the drivers needed a lot of skill, but the 'Duchesses' would work quite happily in the steam locomotive equivalent of fourth gear at 70mph (providing the fireman was up to the task!) and even better if driven to use the minimum amount of steam possible. Whether by accident or design, this tolerance on the part of the locomotive to indifferent driving meant that they were quickly adored by drivers from London to Glasgow, and that's always an acid test for a locomotive.

And finally, there's the appearance of the 'Duchesses'. In their original streamlined form, which Stanier memorably described as a 'carapace', they looked stunning. The cleanliness of their lines, with few protrusions, and that smoothly rounded front end, looked much more aerodynamic than their 'A4' rivals on the East Coast Main Line, and even today it will look modern on *Duchess of Hamilton* – so much so that you could paint one in the red and silver colours of Virgin Trains and park it in one of the platforms at Euston without it looking out of place. But it's their unstreamlined appearance that epitomises the qualities of the 'Duchesses' to me. It would have been easy for Coleman and Stanier to have made them appear rather ungainly, perhaps even vulgar. As for a dedicated bodybuilder, with such big locomotives, it was impossible to disguise their bulk, but by keeping the design as clean and simple as possible, they put this bodybuilder of a locomotive design into a dinner suit, and the result was magnificent. From the hunkered-down way the smokebox rests at the front, to the gentle taper of the boiler, the sloped sides of the firebox and their imposing cabs, the unstreamlined 'Duchesses' have a powerful presence, but it's not an unfriendly one. If anything, a 'Duchess' always reminds me of a shire horse, an effect amplified by the addition of the smoke deflecting plates at the front, which look like blinkers on a horse. They look like gentle giants, and that's the impression I've gained of them from talking to people who worked on them, yet at speed on a long train, a 'Duchess' is a rather different spectacle, the shire horse seemingly transformed into a racing thoroughbred, but still the essential gentleness of the design remaining.

The 'Duchesses' ruled the rails for something like twenty-five years, but perhaps the most striking thing is that they continue to do so. Other designs have approached their best performances, but none have matched them, which begs the question as to why the 'Duchesses' aren't regarded much more highly outside the realms of rail enthusiasts: they deserve to be held in the same awe as Concorde, in my view.

I think the answer lies in the assertion that every actor needs a stage, because that of the 'Duchesses' was very different from that of the other great transport icons. Whether it's *Flying Scotsman* standing at the head of a train at King's Cross, or Concorde taking off at full power from Heathrow, or the *QE2* departing Southampton, all the other transport icons involve a fanfare at arrival or departure. The 'Duchesses' were different. There was no Hollywood glitz and glamour in the climbs to Shap and Beattock summits, no spectacle of being revered by adoring crowds. It was a much more intimate, more human spectacle of men and machine pitting their wits and their strength against nature. Even today, Shap and Beattock aren't easy places to reach if you want to watch trains, and back in steam days, despite there being many more stations on the line, they were even harder. The 'Duchesses' performed to the hills and crags of the Lake District and lowland Scotland rather than to huge crowds, only those few passengers on the train with any interest understanding what was going on at the front, and of the sinews – flesh and steel – being strained to get them over the hills.

It's a shame because the story of the 'Duchesses' deserves to be better known. From *Coronation*'s 114mph record, to *Duchess of Abercorn*'s huge power outputs and the way they outperformed the diesels, it's a tale of intelligence, courage, skill and strength – and the exploits of *Duchess of Hamilton* and *Duchess of Sutherland* in preservation only amplify just what a cracking design they are. In the coming years, we could have *Duchess of Hamilton* and *Duchess of Sutherland* running on the main line, looking very different, but still in a league of their own. Were they the ultimate? All things considered, it remains exceedingly difficult to argue against them being so. They may not have been the most versatile or efficient locomotives ever built, but when it came to the crunch, a 'Duchess' would haul trains that no other locomotives could at speeds they couldn't match – and with the achievements of railway preservation seemingly boundless, who knows, perhaps the best is still to come.

Acknowledgements

As always, there's a host of people who have given their time, knowledge and experience to help produce the book.

First, Brian Radford, Brell Ewart and the volunteers of the Princess Royal Class Locomotive Trust, who have spent long hours sharing what it is to buy, overhaul, maintain and operate a big steam locomotive on the main line. Special thanks must be given to the Trust's excellent curator, Kate Smith, who has answered all my myriad questions with patience and good humour at all times.

The train timing expert Mike Notley has been brilliant, describing the events of the 1980s and early 1990s (which as a child then I don't remember much about when it comes to main-line steam) and providing some stunning analysis of the performances of *Duchess of Hamilton* and *Duchess of Sutherland* that's nearly as thrilling to read as it must have been to experience at first hand.

Many people from Crewe wrote, telephoned or emailed about their experiences with the 'Duchesses', and I'd particularly like to thank Harold Fortuna, Les Jackson, Geoff Hillyard and all the other people who took time to contact me. If their experiences haven't been used, they have certainly informed me much more thoroughly and I've valued them all.

Nigel Harris, my old boss on *RAIL*, and former editor of *Steam Railway*, has been helpful and supportive throughout the book's genesis, and his tale of how the steam-hauled Royal Train started is one that probably deserves greater recognition than it otherwise has received. Likewise, another former editor of *Steam Railway*, Tony Streeter, has provided a great deal of informed opinion about the re-streamlining of *Duchess of Hamilton*.

Thanks to Ian Wild, who helped me research the book, to my colleagues on *International Railway Journal*, and Tim Naylor for helping calculate some of the figures (maths isn't my strong point and I was glad of the help). To David, Keith, Jennifer and Fiona on IRJ, for coping with short-notice absences to interview people, and to my fiancée, Jenny, for her patience and tolerance of the late nights, early starts, and thinking aloud the book has prompted.

To anyone and everyone who I've failed to mention for your help and contributions, I do apologise – but I have genuinely and sincerely valued your input.

Final thanks are due to my publisher at Aurum Press, Graham Coster, whose help, support and encouragement marks him out as one of publishing's true gentlemen, and to my editor, Andrew Grice, who has burnished the copy to the state it is in: if there are any errors in the book, the fault is mine, and mine alone – do visit my website at www.andrewroden.com if you'd like to get in touch with any feedback or comments.

Bibliography

Allen, C.J., *The Locomotive Exchanges 1870–1948*, Ian Allan Publishing, 1949

Allen, C.J., *British Pacific Locomotives*, Ian Allan Publishing, 1962

Bellwood, John and Jenkinson, David, *Gresley and Stanier: A Centenary Tribute*, HMSO, 1976

Blakemore, Michael and Rutherford, Michael, *46229 Duchess of Hamilton*, Friends of the National Railway Museum, 1984

Butcher, Alan C. (ed), *Railways Restored*, Ian Allan Publishing, 2008

Chacksfield, J.E., *Sir William Stanier: A new biography*, Oakwood Press, 2001

Doherty, D. (ed), *The LMS Duchesses*, Model and Allied Publications, 1973

Ewart, Brell and Radford, Brian, *6233 Duchess of Sutherland and the Princess Coronation Class*, PRCLT, 2002

Hale, Don, *Mallard: How the 'Blue Streak' Broke the World Speed Record*, Aurum Press, 2005

Jenkinson, David, *Profile of the Duchesses*, Oxford Publishing Company, 1982

Johnson, P.G., *Through the Links at Crewe*, Xpress Publishing, unknown

Longworth, Hugh, *British Railway Steam Locomotives 1948–1968*, Oxford Publishing Co, 2005

Mullay, A.J., *Streamlined Steam: Britain's 1930s Luxury Expresses*, David & Charles, 1994

Ransome-Wallis, P., *The Last Steam Locomotives of British Railways*, Guild Publishing/Ian Allan Publishing, 1987

Roden, Andrew, *Flying Scotsman: The Extraordinary Story of the World's Most Famous Train*, Aurum Press, 2007

Scott, Peter, *A History of the Butlin's Railways*, Peter Scott, 2001

Sixsmith, Ian, *The Book of the Coronation Pacifics*, Irwell Press, 1998

Uncredited, *L.M. Pacifics: A Pictorial Tribute*, Roundhouse Books, 1967

Whitehouse, P., and Thomas, D.St J., *LMS 150*, David & Charles, 1987

Periodicals

The Railway Magazine
RAIL
Heritage Railway
Steam Railway
Trains Illustrated
Railway World

Videos

Passenger Trains of the LMS, Railfilms, 2008
Steam Memories, Railfilms
Just for the Record, Railfilms

Technical Information

LMS 'Princess Coronation' ('Duchess')
Length: 73ft 10.25in
Weight: locomotive 108.1 tons (streamlined), 105.25 tons
(non-streamlined); tender: 56.35 tons
Height: 13ft 2in
Tractive effort: 40,000lb
Boiler diameter: 6ft 5.5in
Boiler length: 20ft 3in
Boiler pressure: 250psi
Grate area: 50 square feet
Coal capacity: 10 tons
Water capacity: 4,000 gallons (refilled via water troughs)

Class history

Number	Name	Built	Withdrawn	Scrapped/preserved?
6220	*Coronation*	06/37	04/63	05/63
6221	*Queen Elizabeth*	06/37	05/63	07/63
6222	*Queen Mary*	06/37	10/63	01/63
6223	*Princess Alice*	07/37	10/63	10/63
6224	*Princess Alexandra*	07/37	10/63	10/63
6225	*Duchess of Gloucester*	05/38	10/64	12/64
6226	*Duchess of Norfolk*	05/38	10/64	02/65
6227	*Duchess of Devonshire*	06/38	12/62	11/63
6228	*Duchess of Rutland*	06/38	10/64	12/64
6229	*Duchess of Hamilton*	09/38	02/64	Preserved at NRM, York

6230	Duchess of Buccleuch	07/38	11/63	12/63
6231	Duchess of Atholl	07/38	12/62	11/63
6232	Duchess of Montrose	07/38	12/62	11/63
6233	Duchess of Sutherland	07/38	02/64	Preserved at PRCLT, Swanwick Junction
6234	Duchess of Abercorn	08/38	01/63	06/63
6235	City of Birmingham	07/39	10/64	Preserved at Thinktank, Birmingham
6236	City of Bradford	07/39	03/64	04/64
6237	City of Bristol	08/39	10/64	12/64
6238	City of Carlisle	09/39	10/64	12/64
6239	City of Chester	09/39	10/64	12/64
6240	City of Coventry	03/40	10/64	12/64
6241	City of Edinburgh	04/40	09/64	02/65
6242	City of Glasgow	05/40	10/63	11/63
6243	City of Lancaster	06/40	10/64	08/65
6244	King George VI	07/40	10/64	12/64
6245	City of London	06/43	10/64	12/64
6246	City of Manchester	08/43	01/63	05/63
6247	City of Liverpool	09/43	06/63	07/63
6248	City of Leeds	10/43	09/64	11/64
6249	City of Sheffield	04/44	11/63	12/63
6250	City of Lichfield	05/44	10/64	12/64
6251	City of Nottingham	06/44	11/63	12/63
6252	City of Leicester	06/44	06/63	09/63
6253	City of St. Albans	09/46	01/63	05/63
6254	City of Stoke-on-Trent	09/46	10/64	12/64
6255	City of Hereford	10/46	10/64	12/64
6256	Sir William A. Stanier, F.R.S.	12/47	10/64	12/64
46257	City of Salford	05/48	10/64	01/65

Index